LEARNING TO
COACH

LEARNING TO
COACH

For Personal and Professional Development

Nicola Stevens

howto**books**

Published by How To Books Ltd,
Spring Hill House, Spring Hill Road,
Begbroke, Oxford OX 5 1RX, United Kingdom.
Tel: (01865) 375794, Fax: (01965) 379162
info@howtobooks.co.uk
www.howtobooks.co.uk

How To Books greatly reduce the carbon footprint of their books
by sourcing their typesetting and printing in the UK.

First published 2005
Second edition 2008

British Library Cataloguing in Publication Data
A catalogue record for this book is available from the British Library.

Produced for How To Books by Deer Park Productions, Tavistock
Typeset by Kestrel Data, Exeter, Devon
Cover design by Baseline Arts Ltd, Oxford
Printed and bound by Cromwell Press Ltd, Trowbridge, Wiltshire

978 1 84528 271 4

NOTE: The material contained in this book is set out in good
faith for general guidance and no liability can be accepted
for loss or expense incurred as a result of relying in particular
circumstances on statements made in the book. Laws and
regulations are complex and liable to change, and readers should
check the current position with the relevant authorities before
making personal arrangements.

Contents

List of illustrations   ix
Preface   xi
Acknowledgements   xiii

Introduction: What is Coaching?   **1**
  Background of coaching   1
  Welcome to the world of coaching!   3
  Get the best out of *Becoming a Coach*   5
  Definition of Coaching   5
  Diversity   9
  Levels of Coaching   11
  Commissioning coaching   14

1 Preparing Yourself to be an Effective Coach   **17**
  Coaching qualities, competencies and skills   17
  Core coaching competencies   21
  Coaching skills   23
  The coach's own training and development   48
  Supervision for coaches   50
  Self-assessment of the coaching session   51
  Self-management for the coach   52
  In summary   55

2 Building the Coaching Relationship and Managing Client's
    Expectations   **56**
  Managing expectations   56
  Finding the right coach   58
  Personality style   60

Personal working styles   62
Differing learning styles   65
The purpose of coaching   67
Referring prospective clients   70
Barriers to learning and experience   71
Seeking additional help   73
Putting things on hold   74
Putting clients in the picture   75
In summary   76

3   Creating the Foundation of the Coaching Relationship   77
Different coaching styles   77
Getting to know your client   78
Setting objectives   79
Safe and courageous coaching space   80
Co-designing and logistics of the coaching relationship   83
The five viewpoints of future life   85
Goals and primary focus for coaching   101
Responsibility of coach and coachee   103
In summary   105

4   The Coaching Process   106
Creating balance   106
Models for coaching   108
Process of learning   112
Facilitate planning   114
Preparations for coaching   116
Remaining impartial   118
Provide a sustainable relationship   120
Learning from action and experience   122
The three 'A's of re-learning   123
Recognising personality types   123
Recognising gremlin behaviour   124
Finding the reality   126
Maintaining flexibility   127
Utilising life skills   129
Closure   130

Completing the coaching session   131
Concluding the coaching relationship   133
After-care service   133
In summary   134

5 Third Party or Sponsored Coaching Programmes   135
Defining the manager and the internal coaching role   136
Using internal and external professional coaches   138
Issues of accountability, responsibility and authority   140
Confidentiality and expectations within organisations   142
How to prepare and run an organisational coaching
        programme   142
Logistics   144
A springboard session for a sponsored coachee   144
Individual, team and group coaching   145
Coaching groups and teams   146
Concluding the coaching relationship   147
Setting up a mentoring programme for sustainable
        professional development   148
Measurement of success   149
In summary   152

6 Setting Yourself Up as a Coach   153
Finding your coaching style   153
Five easy steps to a sustainable and profitable coaching
        business   154
Tips and traps of coaching   158
Frequently asked questions about coaching   163
Measurement of coaching   166
Setting ethics, standards, terms and conditions   168
Forms and toolkit for coaching   170

Resources   186
Glossary   193
Bibliography and Further Reading   201
Index   205

List of Illustrations

1   Steps to coaching relationship and key phrases of coaching process   4

2   Soft skills used in coaching   7

3   Directive or non directive styles of organisational and individual coaching   11

4   Sample of personal qualities of coaches   19

5   Template of personal qualities of coaches   20

6   Templete of coaching competencies   22

7   Four key phases of coaching process   23

8   The five key coaching skills   24

9   Coaching skill 1 – Rapport   25

10   Coaching skill 2 – Listening   28

11   Coaching skill 3 – Questioning   33

12   Coaching skill 4 – Communication   39

13   Coaching skill 5 – Learning and experience   42

14   Wheel of self-management skills   53

15   Wheel of self-caring management   54

16   The interaction and flow of the coaching relationship energies   57

17   Creating the springboard – 1st key phase of coaching process   78

18   Example of completed Wheel of Life   89

19   Keeping the focus on the client's broader purpose by
       balancing big and little agendas   107

20   Process of learning   112

21   Facilitate planning – 2nd key phase of coaching process   113

22   The coaching process grows from the coachee's own
       qualities and style   118

23   Provide a sustainable relationship – 3rd key phase of
       coaching process   120

24   The cycle of learning and experience during the coaching
       process   121

25   The pendulum of new learning to achieve the desired
       results   123

26   Closure – 4th key phase of the coaching process   130

27   Wheel template   171

Preface

To be asked to update Learning to Coach has given me the great satisfaction of being able to respond to the many enquiries I have received about coaching and its use. These range from 'What is coaching?', 'How do you become a coach?' and 'How can you measure the effectiveness of coaching?' to running seminars and debates on 'What is executive coaching?' and 'Is there a role in modern management?'

I have monitored the journey taken by others to become an effective coach in the personal or professional development arena. It takes time, practical and theoretical learning, supervision, commitment and personal awareness. As part of this process, readers wrote to share the benefits from a framework here to guide them, together with a repertoire of skills, resources and though-provoking questions to form a personal context of effective coaching.

This book has been written based on my own experiences – as a coach and being coached over the past decade by others from differing professional backgrounds, cultures, experience and training. It has been expanded to cover the issues of 3rd party sponsorship coaching in more detail. It still remains very important for anyone offering coaching skills and tools to know what it feels like to be coached. The highs, lows, plateaus, 'I feel stuck' and 'Ah ah moments'. There are specifically devised coaching homework and exercises to follow that aid this process and gives the reader an understanding of coaching and its impact.

In addition, many of my colleagues have been generous with sharing their experience of setting up coaching businesses and working within this new and expanding profession. I wish to thank them, Dan Midwinter for his graphic and technical help and Giles Lewis and Nikki Read at How To Books.

Nicola Stevens

Contact details:
email: ns@proactivecoaching.com
Website: www.proactivecoaching.com
+44 (0)20 7470 8733

Acknowledgements

To the special group of clients who agreed to have their coaching process used as living histories of the coaching qualities, competencies and skills required to create and sustain the coaching process. Also, to the coaches who gave me insights to their experiences, strengths and hopes for the coaching profession.

All their names have been changed, but their contributions have helped keep the guidance and learning in this book, fresh and alive for its readers.

Introduction:
What is Coaching?

BACKGROUND OF COACHING

Coaching, applied to the broader horizon of life, is a relatively new profession. The concept of an older, wiser person imparting their wisdom and learning for the development of a pupil – a mentoring/teaching role – is steeped in history and the basis for many myths and fairy tales throughout the world. More recently, the concept of coaching has been employed and accepted as normal in the sports arena. A sports coach is someone who has experience of sporting discipline and brings out the best in a player – often beyond pure technical skills.

The profession of coaching in the 21st century has built on these foundations. By extending and refining basic principles, the profession has created a discipline that focuses on the process of lifelong learning and development throughout all aspects of people's personal and professional lives. Coaching acknowledges that all areas of life – career, money, health, family and friends, partner, personal growth, recreation and physical environment – are all interlinked, creating either balance or unbalance, depending on the sustainability of actions within each area.

Although coaching is a process that encourages lifelong learning, the discipline is not based on a dependent relationship. Coaching is about unlocking a person's potential to maximize their own performance. It is helping them to learn and understand their experiences rather than teaching them. Coaching is not about the coach knowing it all, giving advice and 'fixing' the client (or 'coachee'), neither is it a friendly chat and collusion of behaviours.

The coach creates a safe, non-judgemental environment in which the coachee can reflect, review, plan action, move forward and learn from the experience. The skills, tools, talent and techniques that a coach needs to develop are all interconnected. This coaching knowledge creates an environment, together with a high level of meaningful language, trust and understanding, that is unique to each partnership and creates maximum value to each client.

This book has been written as a guide for would-be coaches, those working in the personal and professional development arena and anyone using coaching in their everyday life. Many people use coaching skills as part of their day-to-day activities, in addition to those who coach professionally in an internal or external capacity – such as managers, teachers, leaders and volunteers.

Learning to Coach helps to identify the critical issues of responsibility, accountability and authority that are involved in the coaching process. Such issues emerge during any relationship that uses a coaching style – for example between managers and their team or professional coaches and their client. Anyone wishing to offer coaching to others needs specific coaching training – whether they are already qualified in a complementary field (for example, a highly trained therapist), a successful executive wishing to coach at Board level or a volunteer offering to coach young people. Coaching is a profession in its own right and this book gives a thorough explanation of coaching skills and interactions, and highlights possibilities for further training and development. It also sets the place coaching fills in the arena of professional and personal life long learning and achievement.

Coaching is an accepted international profession, which is now imbedded in many different cultures and languages. *Learning to Coach* gives an insight into how coaching is employed in given situations and what makes the coaching process successful, valuable and worthwhile, however diverse the circumstances may be. In addition, the book goes beyond the issues of delivering coaching – by highlighting the importance of building a coaching relationship that ensures a sustainable, energetic, ongoing coaching process. By reading this book you will begin to know what to expect from coaching and make judgements about the experience – whether you are the coach or the coachee.

WELCOME TO THE WORLD OF COACHING!

Learning to Coach has identified three steps to accomplish a valuable coaching relationship. These are:

Step 1 – Initial contact
Step 2 – Foundation of the coaching relationship
Step 3 – The coaching process

These three steps are interwoven with four key phases of the coaching process:

Key phase one – Create the springboard for meaningful coaching
Key phase two – Facilitate planning
Key phase three – Provide a sustainable relationship
Key phase four – Closure

Chapter 1 guides the reader through the process of identifying coaching qualities, competencies and skills, highlighting learning and development.

Chapter 2 assesses the process and the opportunities of the initial client contact.

Chapter 3 reviews the foundations of the coaching relationship and identifies the elements that create a powerful springboard from which the coaching process can begin.

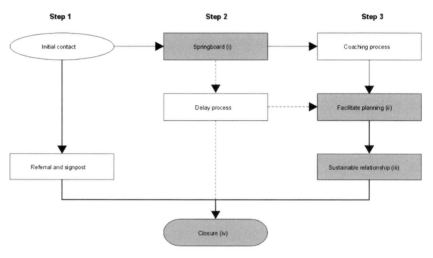

Fig. 1.   Steps to coaching relationship and key phases of coaching process.

Chapter 4 steps through the ongoing process of sustaining a valuable coaching experience.

Chapter 5 defines the role of coaching sponsored by a third party, looking at issues such as setting up a coaching programme, and the difference between working with internal and external coaches, individuals, teams and groups.

Chapter 6 outlines the practicalities of setting up a coaching practice and underlines the necessities of aligning a coaches own values and style to their coaching method.

GET THE BEST OUT OF *LEARNING TO COACH*

To experience and reinforce the learning in this book '**Coaching Homework**' has been specifically designed throughout each chapter to 1) practise skills and learn from the experience, and 2) focus on your own coaching development and style.

To gain a professional outlook and benefit from the learning experience, your practice clients need to be detached from your close circle of family and friends. You could choose a colleague at work, someone you have met at the gym or someone that has been recommended by a friend. Ask around.

You need to make it clear that – whatever the coaching objectives and aims are – you will be working with your client as a whole person, with a wide and varied lifestyle. Preoccupations with work can often have an effect on home and social life. Difficulties in one's personal life may also be reflected in the workplace. You must remember that personal behaviours, values, attitudes, barriers, future desires and experiences are echoed throughout all areas of life and will have a co-responding affect on a client's immediate world. Your clients need to know that too.

DEFINITION OF COACHING

There are many snappy definitions of coaching – quick 60-second 'elevator' speeches and 'audio logos' are available to explain what coaching is and what it can do for the client, usually in relation to what the coach wants to (or is prepared to) offer.

The reasons for undertaking coaching, the methods used and the results achieved are unique to every individual. However, the fundamental philosophy of coaching is contained within the following simple, clear definition:

Coaching is a **relationship** that is designed in such a way as to enhance the process of lifelong **learning, effectiveness** and **fulfilment.**

Identifying the difference

What is the difference between coaching and other forms of personal and professional development?

The question 'what is coaching?' often results in a series of explanations that try to give coaching a meaningful value or possible benefit. These explanations often cloud the understanding of coaching.

Recently, at a party, the following conversation took place between two guests meeting for the first time.

'Hi . . . So, I work in pharmaceuticals. What do you do?'
'Oh – I'm a coach'.
'Oh, you coach sports – great. What sports do you coach?'
'No – I work with individuals and organisations in whatever area or issues they would like to focus on to enhance their lives and potential'.
'Okay – Is that like therapy?'
'No . .'.
'Oh, you mean life coaching – like in woman's magazines?'

Before the conversation had finished, coaching had been likened to a voice coach, mentoring and then finishing with:

'Oh – you're a consultant then?'

The coach felt stumped and quickly changed the conversation to another subject.

Coaching has become a modern buzzword, and as a result coaching has often been misrepresented in the professional arena. There are several ways to train as a coach or to become involved in other developmental arenas, such as therapy, counselling, mentoring, training and consulting. Many of the same soft skills are used across the development arenas. They are related to people skills, i.e. behaviour or state of mind. Hard skills are related to technical expertise i.e. accounting or law.

Sometimes coaching jargon is used in a variety of professions to illustrate validity or jazz old themes. This has tended to dilute the power and real value of the professional coaching process. In turn, it also muddies the water of the value and expertise of other developmental practices.

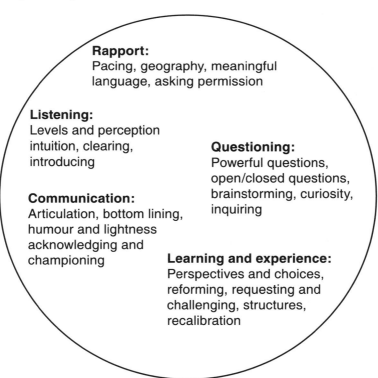

Fig. 2. Soft skills used in coaching.

Therapy/Counselling

'The overall aim of counselling is to provide an opportunity for the client to work towards living in a way he or she experiences as more satisfying and resourceful.'

The British Association of Counselling and Psychotherapy (BACP), taken from *Learning to Counsel* by Jan Sutton and William Stewart.

Therapy is used in times of personal crisis, where resolution is based on a re-examination of the past in order to make the patient feel whole, resourceful and creative in their own right. Coaching starts from the point that all coachees are already naturally creative, resourceful and whole. As one coach put it, there tends to be 'a sadness' involved in therapeutic work, such as bereavement. The following examples of therapy juxtaposed coaching words help to illustrate the differences between these two disciplines:

Therapy	*Coaching*
Why me/why this?	What's next/what now?
Overcoming obstacles	Sustainable flow
Looks back	Raising standards
Somewhat vulnerable	Actively building
Needs help	Frustration
Pain	Present/future
Professional arm's length	Uniqueness
Healing of emotion	Related experiences
Damage	Missed opportunities
Restoration	Unlimited scope

Mentoring

Mentoring is traditionally associated with a more experienced person guiding and passing on their knowledge and experience to others. The mentee could be following in their mentor's footsteps or using them as a role model. The modern twist to this is the 'reverse mentoring process'. This is a relationship in which a younger person has experience that they can share with the older generation – such as IT technology. Essentially mentoring is about sharing knowledge and experience. The mentoring model has been revised to also enable open lines of communication and innovation within organisations through peer and buddy mentoring programmes.

Training

Training is used when a skill – whether situational, theoretical or practical – needs to be taught. Examples of training-related activities include using new IT software, learning how to cook or learning to use a new managerial process at work. The information is taught in a prescriptive mode.

Consultants

Consultants are used for the skills and experience that they can impart in a given situation. Consultants can give specific advice to an individual about the options available and the pros and cons of the choices they make. You hire a consultant to advise you how to go about a process.

DIVERSITY – DIFFERENCES AND SIMILARITIES

The profession of coaching is practised worldwide and therefore across many differing cultures and lives. Some coaches will decide that they would like to work within a niche area of clients. This could include nationality, language or situational experience. Business and social factors have opened up access to providing coaching 24/7 globally and the newly announced diversity policy in Europe is based on six pillars which are gender, ethnicity, ageism, disability, religion and sexual orientation. Acknowledging diversity, differences and similarities has become a requirement in the coaching arena.

For many coaches, the greatest challenges come with language and social expectations. Coaching has primarily grown using the language of US English. Thus transferring skills, meaning and experience directly into another language brings its own set of misunderstandings. For example, when teaching coaching skills to a group of Russian businessmen about the process of learning, the direct translation of the four steps of the learning process (*see page 112, Figure 20*) caused great concern. The word 'competence' had a negative meaning for them. The translation of competence from unconscious incompetence through to unconscious competence had no change in understanding for them. After a discussion between the translator, the English coach teaching them the soft skills and the Russian businessmen themselves, it was decided the wording should be changed to 'unconscious lack of knowledge' through to 'unconscious known knowledge'. Knowledge as a word had a positive meaning for them, which fitted the meaning intended by the original English. Instances like this have therefore brought fresh – and exciting – challenges to the practice of coaching.

In other regions, creating and using a coaching model for the motivation and continuous learning for employees and individuals is desirable, but also needs to be sensitive to the backdrop of the business, family or social culture. Ideas regarding what is creating potential in a person's life may differ in understanding and need. Those who are living a more basic lifestyle will have differing wants and needs to those in more privileged positions. This may sound very obvious, but it is surprising how many coaches can get caught up in the mode of bringing the best potential out in their clients while forgetting to service and understand the basic needs of coachees. Such keen coaches can get bogged down in coaching models and will try to teach their jargon to clients, rather than being flexible and happy to explore what has the greatest relevance and meaning for coachees that they can continue to use when the coaching sessions are completed. Maslow's hierarchy of needs, originally illustrated in the 1950s, is still relevant today for explaining the motivations and expectations of differing societies.

In the following chapter coaching skills are explored more fully. Under the headings of creating and maintaining 'rapport' and verbal and non verbal 'listening', it is essential to build a solid foundation of understanding from which to further build a coaching relationship that allows for an on-going recalibration of both understanding and meaning between the coach and the coachee.

LEVELS OF COACHING – INFORMAL TO LINE MANAGER TO PROFESSIONAL COACH

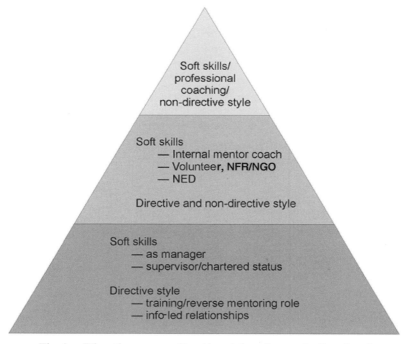

Fig. 3. Directive or non-directive styles of organisational and individual coaching.

The directive and non-directive ways in which skills are deployed by coaches have a significant impact on the process and outcome of coaching. It also makes a difference if the coaching process is informal or formal. An informal coaching relationship usually works on an ad hoc basis, with the coaching process based on a regular meeting programme. However, some professional coaches offer an aftercare service to former clients which enables the latter to have access to a coaching session should they need one. Informal coaching generally happens within the workplace where there is no regular coaching programme, with managers choosing to coach their teams when they think it is needed rather than on a regular basis or via internal coaches run a coaching clinic. Factors influencing the differing approaches are governed by the nature of the relationship between coach and coachee. This is always a relationship of accountability, responsibility and authority. Professional coaches will set up formal coaching relationships based on the needs and agendas of their clients.

Directive style coaching

The bottom third of the triangle in Figure 3 shows situations when a directive style of soft skills is used in coaching. These skills would be for training, mentoring models, and managers and supervisors of some educational programmes for chartered status in professions such as law, accountancy and the building sector. For example, if a coach is the line manager of a coachee they will come to a point where the manager will be directive about actions and goals. While they may not have a preference over how a project is completed, they do need to see certain goals achieved. However, the manager may also want the coachee to learn certain elements and practices in the workplace for their professional development, and in order to gain the necessary training to achieve this, the manager, as coach, will need to be directive about the process irrespective of their coachees' willingness. The main influences that drive achievement are organisational aims and objectives, not personal goals and motivation. This is a directive use of coaching skills.

Directive and non directive style

Following Figure 3 through to the middle part of the diagram there will be occasions when both a directive and a non directive style may be used. This could be the internal coach who trains and mentors managers on skills for managing teams and performance, or a Non-Executive Director (NED) whose position on the board means that they are balancing being a non-directive sounding board for the executive board, or being directive in the strategic direction of the organisation. Again, this can be the case within the voluntary sector where there are both paid officers and volunteers working together and sharing responsibilities for the effectiveness of an organisation. Depending on the relationship and motivation of both coach and coachee, it would be easier to use a directive style with paid officers to accomplish goals rather than with volunteers who need to be engaged in their performance and motivated to give their time and expertise free, and are therefore usually happy for backing with a non-directive supportive style. There can be occasions, however, when internal coaches within organisations, however much they try, will have issues with being totally non-directive in a coaching relationship. Here they have a duty to their employer and their own employee performance to maintain. This creates a conflict of interest. However good in-house coaching programmes are they are often tainted, rightly or wrongly, with being recorded in some way on employees' HR records. This then makes the coaching process seem unsafe and less than confidential.

Non-directive style

The top section of the triangle in Figure 3 represents the use of soft skills by professional coaches. These coaches will have spent many hundreds of hours of supervised training and will have committed themselves to continual professional development (CPD) and regular supervision. A coach who works at this level will only use a non-directive style and will usually be external to the organisation or in no way connected to the coachee. The coaching agenda and aims will be the client's – the coachee – and will not be influenced by the coach. If the coach feels that there is an issue with the coaching relationship they can end it immediately.

The hierarchy of position and power that a coach might have over a coachee also affects the balance of accountability and responsibility that is expected within the relationship.

COMMISSIONING COACHING

Many coaches carve out a niche so that they can market themselves according to the types of clients they would like to have and their existing contacts and experience. Although the list of specialist and niche coaching is endless, the commissioning of coaching can be split into two groups – 1st party coaching and 3rd party/sponsor coaching.

1st party coaching

1st party coaching is a direct relationship between individuals and their choice of coach. Individuals choose to be coached around issues that they currently have, or need to consider, in order to find an even more satisfying lifestyle (or simply to reflect where they are now). This could include looking at work/life balance, a future career path, life purpose, values, wants and wishes. 1st party coaching is future focused and totally centred around the client's agenda.

Occasionally, a friend, family member or spouse may suggest that an individual seeks coaching for a particular issue. This is a form of 3rd party coaching, because another person has expressed an interest in the coaching process. 3rd party coaching can compromise a client's agenda. For this reason it is important to acknowledge that two of the cornerstones for a valuable, productive coaching relationship are confidentiality and coaching on a client driven agenda – not an imposed agenda.

3rd party/sponsor coaching

Some organisations commission a coach to work with individuals or groups in order to explore business-related topics and to support employees in their positions. The organisation may have some specific areas that they would like their employees to be coached on. However, an accepted ethos of coaching is that it is a holistic process – therefore coaching can focus on both personal and business issues to complement the objectives of the organisation and the personal motivations of the individual.

It is worth taking a moment to acknowledge the power and effect that personal life, motivations and aspirations have on professional and business lives. To gain the maximum value, a 3rd party/sponsored coaching programme must include the personal goals that an individual has expressed in the foundation session. Failure to do so will dilute the permanent success of coaching objectives. See Chapter 5 – Third Party Coaching Programmes.

Coaching for coaches

It is very important for anyone using coaching skills and tools to know what it feels like to be coached. The highs, lows, plateaus, 'I feel stuck' and the 'Ah ha!' moments. If a coach has never experienced these situations, they will never be able to empathise with the feelings of their client during the coaching process.

Coaching can be used in the following ways:

♦ A stand alone development tool in its own right for personal and professional learning

♦ In conjunction with a training process to reinforce and imbed the learning

♦ A proactive process to assess and reflect on personal and professional possibilities.

Three methods of coaching are:

♦ Face to face

♦ Telephone

♦ Email and other technologically driven media. For example, Skype, webeminars or chat rooms for live email exchange. These advances in technology help to overcome issues of disability, remote working or flexitime working and enable coaches to offer more cost effective ways of delivering sessions to clients.

Such methods are usually supported by email and telephone contact and support between booked coaching appointments. Some coaches offer both face-to-face and telephone coaching, other coaches choose to specialise in one or the other.

Coaches running their own practice (or those using coaching skills in their everyday life) need to choose a method of coaching that best suits them. *Learning to Coach* will guide you through this process, highlighting the questions you need to ask, and looking at the possibilities that will help you in your decision-making.

1
Preparing Yourself to be an Effective Coach

Coaches come from many different backgrounds, experience and knowledge. In order to assess current transferable abilities and plan development for refreshing or learning new skills, this chapter explores the different elements that are required in professional coaching. These are:

♦ Coaching qualities, competencies and skills

♦ Training and development for coaches

♦ Self-management for coaches.

COACHING QUALITIES, COMPETENCIES AND SKILLS

There are fundamental personal qualities, coaching competencies and skills that are needed to be a good coach – irrespective of whether coaching is being employed externally, internally in the workplace or voluntarily. While exploring the essential coaching characteristics needed, it is important to acknowledge personal qualities, existing competencies and skills learnt through other experiences, in order to build and expand on these areas. This will give a framework to focus on further coaching development and learning.

Being a great coach is not about being a 'personality', but it is about being able to create relationships and work well in collaborative interactions with others. This does not come naturally to everyone, but these qualities can be practised and developed. Just as athletes – who are naturally good at running – need to train their muscles to a higher degree of performance.

Personal qualities

The following personal qualities are useful in the coaching profession:

1) **People person** – being at ease with people and enjoying personal interactions

2) **Empathetic and respectful** – interested in and sensitive to all aspects and complexities of peoples' lives

3) **Collaborative** – able to build a rapport and sustain ongoing relationships and collaborations

4) **Willing** – willing to help others in ways that are supportive to their needs

5) **Self-managed** – open-minded, responsible and able to manage their own lives without negatively affecting others.

Successful coaches have many of these interpersonal skills naturally in their bones. Friends and colleagues would describe them as being 'good with people'. Being successful in business, living life to the full or being the greatest 'sympathetic listener' at work, is not the guarantee of a good coach. Personal qualities – such as being interested in and able to interact easily with people – help a coach to excel naturally in their work.

Having the right personal qualities helps, but an overall balance of strength is needed. Personal qualities can be developed if they are stronger in some areas and weaker in others. Being aware of your own development needs is important. Coaching is not a fad or a quick fix approach solution. Neither is the coach there to give advice, 'sort the problem' or be directive in such a way as to railroad the client. Coaching is a focused, non-dependant, collaborative relationship. The Coaches Training Institute (CTI) describe clients as 'naturally

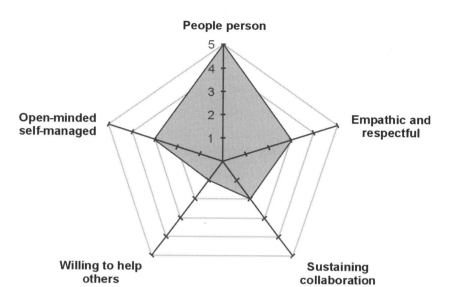

Fig. 4.   Sample of personal qualities of coaches.

creative, resourceful and whole' people – and rarely seek a coach to be 'fixed'.

Working with your client

The client-centred way that coaching works demands a willingness, collaboration, respect and empathy on the coach's part to be able to work in ways that suit the client. Being impatient with coachees who naturally respond to situations in a different way does not make for a valuable coaching experience. This does not mean that the coach needs to collude with bad behaviour, limited thinking or actively encourage erratic actions in keeping with the client's old philosophy of life. However, a coach should refrain from swooping into the relationship like a hawk, identifying areas for improvement from the bird's eye viewpoint, telling the client what to do, how to do it and then spend the following sessions checking the mission is accomplished. A coach needs to maintain good self-management skills.

Coaching is about working with clients in their current situation, not where the coach would like them to be – whether there is a personal resonance with some of the issues raised or not. A coach can always choose whether to work with a client – and set their own boundaries and preferences in relation to the client. This is discussed more fully in Chapter 3 – Creating the Foundation for the Coaching Relationship.

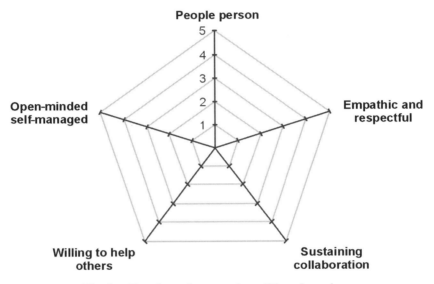

Fig. 5.   Template of personal qualities of coaches.

More importantly, being a coach and helping people is not a substitute for a normal healthy, personal relationship or to satisfy a personal void. Coaches, like the rest of the human race, are not perfect, but they need to be whole, rounded and resourceful – just like the clients who seek coaching to fulfil their needs. The self-management of coaches is more fully explained on page 52.

COACHING HOMEWORK

Using the template on page 20: complete Figure 5 by answering the following questions:

Where do you rate yourself 1–5 (5 being the highest) in naturally having the personal qualities listed?

Ask three people – family/friends/colleagues – to get some objective feedback here – how would they rate you having the personal qualities listed 1–5?

What are the similarities and differences in your own view of your qualities and those marked by others? What do you need to develop?

All coaches need to develop their coaching competencies to become proficient in coaching skills.

CORE COACHING COMPETENCIES

There is a lot of written material about coaching models, and the competencies and skills required to carry them out – all using differing terms and professional jargon. However, there are five core coaching competencies and skills that are known to create great coaching relationships.

These five competencies are:

♦ Professionalism – being able to meet professional ethics, standards and responsibilities

♦ Confidentiality – ensuring total confidentiality and creating a safe, healthy coaching environment

♦ Non-judgemental – being understanding and compassionate to the
client and sensitive to their experience, needs and personal styles

♦ Impact of coaching – appreciating the power and impact of coaching to the client and their life

♦ Collaboration – working openly and in a collaborative manner
with the client at all times.

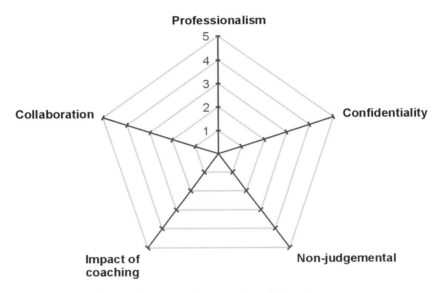

Fig. 6.   Template of personal qualities of coaches.

COACHING HOMEWORK

Complete Figure 6 by answering the following questions:

Where do you rate yourself 1–5 (5 being the highest) in naturally having the
coaching competencies listed?

Ask three people – family/friends/colleagues – to get some objective
feedback here – how would they rate you having the coaching
competencies listed 1–5?

What are the similarities and differences in your own view of your competencies and those marked by others? What do you need to develop?

COACHING SKILLS

There are four key phases that occur in the development of a coaching relationship and a sustainable, ongoing coaching process:

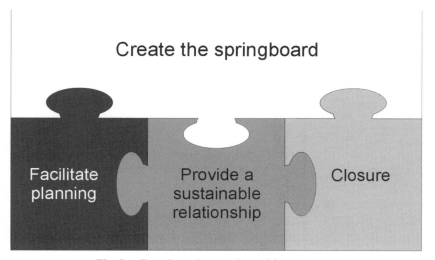

Fig. 7.   Four key phases of coaching process.

(i)   *Creating a springboard* for the coaching relationship that is of value and meaningful to the coach and coachee.

(ii)   *Facilitating planning*, action, results, learning and development that is natural to the coaching process.

(iii) *Providing a sustainable relationship* that is creative, dynamic and productive to support the client's own agenda.

(iv)   *Closure* to complete the current coaching progress, while supporting the client's future if they require further contact and check-up appointments with the coach.

During a coaching session several skills are being used at any one time during the four key phases. One coach has said that a successful coaching session feels to the client like a 'conversation on the sofa'. In other words, a calm, illuminating exchange that leaves the client feeling heard, understood and ready for the next phase of development and learning wherever that leads.

However, whether the coaching session is face to face or over the telephone, the process of coaching is more than a 'cozy chat'. The skills employed by a coach are used in response to a client's needs and humour at a given time. Coaching can be likened to dancing – being in step with each other, but going through several different tempos and styles in one dance. A coach always considers the client's broader picture and agenda while exploring differing avenues and working with the day-to-day issues, ideas, actions and learning that the coachee is experiencing. This 'dance' of skills falls into five categories:

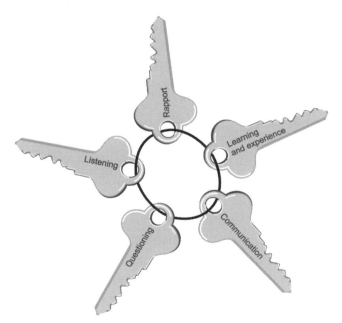

Fig. 8.   The five key coaching skills.

1) Rapport
2) Listening
3) Questions
4) Communication
5) Learning and experience

1. Rapport

Fig. 9.   Coaching skill 1 – Rapport.

Rapport in a coaching relationship can been seen in several ways. For example: in the level of understanding between the coach and coachee; satisfied expectations, outcomes goals and energy levels in the sessions. The skills needed to build and maintaining a healthy rapport between the coach and coachee are:

♦   Pacing

♦   Geography

♦   Meaningful language

♦   Asking permission.

Pacing
One of the most effective ways of building and maintaining rapport is to be able to match aspects of another person. This process (called 'pacing') is an interaction of synchrony that expresses the coach is 'together' with the coachee throughout the whole coaching

process. Pacing forms a bridge between the coach and the client. By acknowledging clients, coaches can build up their trust and so open up all kinds of possibilities to engage with others.

Pacing, however, is not simply copying or mimicry. Rather, it is complementing, harmonising and engaging. For example, what frame of mind does the coachee present – curious, enthusiastic? What are their energy levels like? How does the ambience of the room and the coaches physical position (angle, distance and height) in relation to the coachee affect the rapport?

Geography
A coach needs to recognise their client's 'physical geography' and how they can change it for their client's benefit. Geography is linked to aspects of pacing and includes tone and volume of voice, pace of speech delivery, rates of breathing, body language, positions, and movement – or lack of movement as a reflection of the coachee's mood and humour. For instance, if a client is recounting a situation in a sad monotone voice and explaining that they are tired and unable to achieve anything at the moment, the client will need to change their tone of voice and create body movement to gain a different perspective and energy. This is possible for the coach to achieve by changing their own 'geography' in the session.

Coaches learn how to interpret the effects of geography for the benefit of their client's experience and learning. The coach can help to improve the coaching process by pointing out the geography of their client and requesting they change it. Whether the coaching is face to face or over the telephone there are clues for the coach to be able to understand what attitude of mind and emotional state their client is in and try ways to change it if necessary.

COACHING HOMEWORK

Telephone three friends or work colleagues and judge from the tone of their voice, the kind of language they are using and any other clues, what you think about their current state of mind and attitude to situations.

Ask for feedback from them and see if your insights and theirs correspond.

Meaningful language

All meaningful relationships form their own phrases, jokes and communication shorthand that is only understood by them. For example, Noel Coward in his play *Private Lives* creates the phrase 'Solomon Isaacs' to be used between one of the couples as they felt another argument starting between them. This was reduced to 'Solacs' as the play progresses, but the instant the term was used it has an immediate resonance for the couple. If this level of meaningful language is created from the beginning of a coaching relationship it enables full access to a clear understanding and communication between the coach and coachee. This is explained more fully in Chapter 3 – Creating the Foundation of the Coaching Relationship.

The coach must be aware that different words and phrases mean different things to different people (see page 9 'Diversity'). Some words have a negative or positive effect on us. Coaches often refer to these as 'red' and 'green flag words'. Red flag words are those which have a negative effect and which unintentionally may cause a client to feel defensive, put down or obstructive. Green flag words have a positive effect causing a client to feel encouraged, optimistic and energised.

An unfamiliar context or subject matter can inhibit our understanding of a word, and people usually have a preference for their mode of language. This is sited by Neuro Linguistic Programming (NLP) as Visual, Audio and Kinesthetic modes of language and understanding. For example:

I see what you mean – *Visual*
I hear what you say – *Auditory*
I get the feeling of what you are saying – *Kinesthetic.*

Using the client's mode of communication to interact and reflect back to them helps to build rapport and understanding.

Asking permission
For a coach to truly hold the focus and gain depth in a coaching session, there will undoubtedly be times when subjects are broached or issues raised that cause the client to feel defensive or resistant. If a coach asks permission to continue the exploration of the subject, the client knows that this is being done with their best interests at heart. Whatever the outcome of the discussion, the coach is showing respect to the client. If a coach is given permission to coach through difficult circumstances it is an indication of the degree of trust the coachee feels and the level of confidence guaranteed by the coach.

2. Listening

Fig. 10.   Coaching skill 2 – Listening.

Listening focuses on both the verbal and non-verbal communication that enable 'listening' and an understanding of the intention of what is said and unsaid. There are many ways in which information and meanings can be expressed without words. A lot of research has been undertaken on the meaning of body language but it is part of the human make-up to automatically understand aggressive or friendly body language without knowing the full extent of the subject. The pace, pitch and tone of the voice is a great indicator of emotion and intention. In coaching non-verbal communications is sometimes known as 'observant listening'. Listening skills are:

♦ Listening levels and perception

♦ Intuition

♦ Clearing

♦ Intruding.

Listening levels and perceptions
Coaching is one of the rare times when a client is fully listened to by another person. Sometimes coaching is described as having three person shifts (*Neuro Linguistic Programming* – behavioural flexibility) while other schools of thought describe coaching as having three listening levels (*Co-Active Coaching*).

In the context of coaching:

1st person shift/Level 1 listening is characterised by the direct association and effect that the information is having on the coach or client at the time. For example, the client may be recounting a problematic moment caused by a sudden downpour of rain the day before. The coach starts remembering the rainstorm too and the fact that the drains outside the office overflowed and that subsequent problems resulted. Rather than listening to the client and holding their agenda, the coach is involved in their own related experience and agenda.

2nd person shift/Level 2 listening occurs when the client feels as though they are being 'listened' to. The coach is 'over there' with the client, experiencing the event from the client's perspective. The coach has put themselves in the client's shoes to understand how the rainstorm was experienced and the issues raised by it for their client.

3rd person shift/Level 3 listening occurs when the coach is consciously listening to the client, yet still being aware of themselves and their reactions but in a disassociated way. The coach becomes an observer of the coaching session and uses these observations to be of benefit to the client and to stretch their client's perspective. Even the situation can become a metaphor for the situation the client is in. By listening in a disassociated way about the rainstorm, the coach can point out, 'Wow, that rainstorm literally flooded the event when you were trying to stop flooding your schedule. What's next?'

Listening can be hindered in a number of ways. Blocks to listening include:

♦ **Physical** – for example, external sounds; unpleasant smells; over-crowded room

♦ **Physiological** – for example, disabilities; hearing disorders; illness

♦ **Emotional** – for example, defensiveness; hostility; fear

♦ **Personal** – for example, fatigue; personal problems; hunger; low energy level.

Intuition
Intuition is defined as 'an immediate apprehension by the mind without reasoning'. Intuition is about listening to the coach's 'inner thoughts' and 'flash in their mind's eye' – those gut feelings or flashes of unrelated thoughts that come into the mind that there is something

of truth there, even if you have no evidence. Depending on the personal style of the coach, the intuition may be felt bodily, heard as an internal sound or seen visually. Although intuition has the overtones of something 'spooky', third sight or just plain creepy, it is a very ordinary experience for most people.

Having a hunch or sixth sense about something is a fascinating experience. As a coach, it is surprising the number of times a seemingly 'off the wall' thought suddenly, from nowhere, expresses perfectly what is going on for the client at that time, or illustrates what they would like to achieve. It doesn't happen in every coaching session, but when it resonates with the client it is an enlightening experience. However, to build and use the skill of intuition, coaches need to be prepared to tell the client what they are experiencing and then be unattached to the outcome of how the client receives the information.

COACHING HOMEWORK

Make a telephone call to a friend and note down the mood you think they are in. Note what is being said and what you are reading between the lines. If you get an instant flash of thought as they are speaking (or a visual, audio or physical impression) tell your friend about your intuition and see how they respond.

Clearing
Clearing is a way of dealing with anger, frustration or negativity that can get in the way of coaching. There are occasions when clients come to a coaching session preoccupied by some train of thought or negative feelings. The effect is that the coaching process gets hijacked or over-shadowed and the client is unable to move forward.

In situations like these, the coach needs to take charge and point out to the client what is happening. They may request that the session is suspended temporarily to clear the preoccupations away. The coach then prepares to listen to a major negativity. The coach gives the coachee permission to say whatever they need to, in any fashion they want in order to 'lance' the boiling emotion.

It is important that this activity is time-restricted. Usually this period lasts for 5 or 10 minutes – long enough for the client to vent their anger and frustration, their feelings and thoughts. Throughout this period the coach should encourage the negativity, and ask to hear more of the sorry saga. 'Tell me more' or 'You're sounding very apologetic for being angry – it is safe here. What is really making you angry?' or 'What do you really want to say to them?' Again this is a time when the coach suggests the coachee uses movement to express their feelings.

Clearing shows how deeply the coach is prepared to listen to the coachee. On most occasions a solid period of five minutes venting frustration allows the raw emotion to reach a stage where it can be dealt with effectively. Often the coachee is laughing at the end of the clearing session, and wondering why they were wasting energy on the situation. The coach knows nothing is personally directed at them, but is willing to hold the safe space in service of their client. Clearing can also be used to acknowledge and celebrate successes if it feels necessary to clear the 'space' to move forward in the coaching session.

Intruding
Throughout the coaching process, it is often felt that the client comes first, that a coach must be sensitive to their needs and give them the time and space to judge their own sense of pace and rhythm with which to interact with the coach. However, it is also part of the coach's responsibility to point out and challenge any issues that they see their client avoiding, or generally trying to skirt around issues.

The benefit of establishing a good coaching relationship is that the coach is able to support the life and work visions, dreams, and goals of their client, while still being able to point out any intellectual and emotional incongruency that the client may bring to the coaching that blocks or clouds the reality and issues in hand. The coach should not be afraid to 'point out the elephant standing in the middle of the room' who everyone else is trying to pretend is not there.

A coach needs to learn the skill of intruding and taking charge when they feel their client is digressing within the coaching conversation. One of the questions from the springboard session is for the coach to ask the client how they can best interact with each other in times of difficulty. It takes time, on occasions, for the coach to intrude and take charge, but it is helpful if this situation has already been discussed with the client. To intrude and take charge can be as simple as the coach saying, 'Hey, hold on a moment here . . . !' or 'Wow! That was neatly swept under the carpet'. On other occasions the coach needs to be firmer and be prepared for the client to become defensive, frustrated and angry.

3. Questioning

Fig. 11.   Coaching skill 3 – Questioning.

♦   Powerful questions

♦   Open/Closed questions

♦   Brainstorming

♦   Curiosity

♦   Inquiry.

Powerful questions

The purpose of powerful questions is that they make a client stop and think. These thought processes help a client to find insights and answers to the powerful question they have just been asked and prompt them to access past experiences, knowledge and the innate intuition and inner resources that they have. Powerful questions have been referred to as WAQs (pronounced Whack) – Wisdom Access Questions. Imagine that the brain is one big google search engine. Our brain holds a massive amount of conscious and unconscious memories, experience, learning and information that we have access to, but rarely remember in an instant. Asking powerful questions provides a prompt for the relevant information, rather like using keywords in an internet search engine.

A question is made powerful by starting it with the word 'What' rather than 'Who, Why, When or How'. The 'What' questions forces coachees to be specific in their answers and form of inquiry. For example, if the coachee is asked 'Why are you reading this book?' a client might respond with a story or general answer. If asked, 'What outcome do you want to reach by reading this book?' the client's answer will become future orientated and focused on insights and solutions.

When framing a powerful question, a shorter question is most powerful. As a guideline, approximately seven words or less works best, but longer worded powerful questions can also be effective. A powerful question is direct, focused and easy to understand – even if the question is a difficult one to answer:

'What else in your life is affected by this?'
'What next?'
'What do you want?'
'What is so important about it?'
'What is it to be a leader?'
'What do you need to be?'

'What does it feel like?'

'What else?'

'What is a third option that would take you from between the rock and the hard place?'

Powerfully framed questions get to the heart of the matter – they create possibilities or fresh perspectives for the coachee's learning. However, to spend a whole coaching session just asking powerful questions is exhausting and after a while becomes limiting in itself. A coach needs to use a balance of difference types of questions, including powerful and open questions.

COACHING HOMEWORK

Set yourself a timed period of no less than 30 minutes and practice asking only powerful questions.

What questions did you find most powerful for expanding perspective and learning for your client?

What opportunities in the coaching process did you limit or lose for the benefit of your client by only using powerful questions?

What was the feedback from your client about the questions and the feel of the session for them?

Open/Closed questions

Closed questions tend to be able to be answered with a YES or NO. They do not open up the discussion, or develop thoughts while answering.

Closed question – *'Is this an effective strategy for you?'*

Asking this as an open question inspires creative thinking and encourages a full and more considered answer.

Open question – *'What makes this an effective strategy for you?'*

By turning this into an open question the coach is able to explore more fully what is happening, and broaden the possibilities of the coaching session. Making questions open, encourages the coachee to express more in-depth thoughts and enables them to be shared with the coach, and in some cases, tested for their validity. Sometimes a coachee might interrupt their own answer – 'You know, while I was saying that to you I realised it isn't quite true . . .' Open questions also encourage further exploration and help the client to find the reality and the best way forward. The coach also gets a more complete view, aiding an understanding of the complexities and arousing further questions and thought processes.

Here are some other examples of closed and open questions:

Closed – *'Have you finished your research yet?'*
Open – *'If you had more time, where else would you research?'*

Closed – *'It sounds like you're stuck between two choices – is that true?'*
Open – *'I can see the two obvious choices, but what are the alternative, less obvious options?'*

Brainstorming
Brainstorming (or 'Rainbow Shower' as some people call it) is about creating possibilities that are not restricted by 'shoulds', 'oughts',

rules and regulations. Brainstorming opens up creativity between the coach and coachee and links the impossible to the unrealistic, allowing random and lateral thoughts to blossom so that they gain new perspectives. For example, brainstorming can start with the simple question 'If money were no object – what would you do then?'

There are many ways to kick-start the brainstorming process. For clients who like words, pinpointing words at random from the dictionary or picking a book title and using the essence of the story as way of looking at the coachee's situation bring a creativity, lightness and humour to the coaching session. For example, *The House on the Strand* by Daphne du Maurier is about a man being able to mentally travel back from the 20th century and witness events of his environment in the 13th century. You could ask your client to transpose their situation to the 13th century – 'What would it look like if you were in this same situation in the Dark Ages' or 'How would Captain Kirk in Star Trek fathom your situation out?'

Brainstorming is not a neat logical way to thinking, but it does release the mind to have fun and look at issues and concerns in a free way. It wakes up the brain and shuts down the fear and duty elements of thought to trigger possibilities, different perspectives and choices.

Curiosity
Curiosity is not normally seen as a skill. As children we are often taught that too much curiosity causes problems. There is even a proverb, 'Curiosity killed the cat'. The dictionary definition of being curious is 'to be eager to know and inquisitive' and this is a very powerful tool for a coach to use with their clients. Being curious encourages the coach to be nonjudgemental. Instead of asking 'Why do you want to do something?' (which has overtones of criticism) a coach might say, 'I am curious to know more about what you are achieving.' This style gives the client the opportunity to reflect and examine all

aspects, assumptions and previous experiences that are surrounding their beliefs and actions.

The coach needs to offer a coaching environment that creates insights, challenges assumptions and is a safe place for the client to experience new learning and behaviours. A coach needs to refrain from trying to solve problems – which might make the client feel defensive of their current stance. In cases like this, if the coach reverts to curiosity and states 'I am curious . . .' it gives the coachee the space and freedom to freely examine the current situation.

Inquiry
Inquiry is another form of questioning that the coach and client can use to open up thinking and believing processes. An inquiry is an open-ended question. It is not answered immediately, but is a question to be mulled over a period of time. There is also no logical or linear answer. For instance, a client may be thinking about changing their job and moving to a different location but comes up with lots of reasons of duty that keep them from moving on. Using an inquiry question – 'How would it be if you had no other considerations than to please yourself?' – opens up the field of intellectual thinking, reflection, emotional and spiritual responses for the client.

An inquiring question is a great way to complete a coaching session. The client can consider the inquiry in the time between the next appointment – simply to inquire into themselves and around themselves using the question as a basis for the internal debate. An inquiry is a powerful open question that requires time and reflection to have some sense of understanding – it creates channels of thought way beyond the inquiry itself.

4. Communication

Fig. 12.   Coaching skill 4 – Communication.

The main skills needed in coaching for communication are:

◆   Articulating

◆   Bottom lining

◆   Humour and lightness

◆   Acknowledging and championing.

Articulating

Sometimes a client might hide behind a story. Some clients tell situations through stories as a personal style while others give information in a jumbled, disjointed way because that is how they are thinking of the situation at the time. The coach needs, on these occasions, to articulate what is going on for the client and make sense of the dialogue. It could be that the coach is 'pointing out the elephant in the room', highlighting the oddities and discrepancies that the client is presenting or maybe a case of clearly showing the difficulties that the coach perceives the client is trying to tell them.

The way in which the coach articulates back what they have heard does not have to be rational or make particular sense in the scheme of things, but it can show the client what they are saying to the coach and therefore projecting into the outside world. The coach may choose to mirror the coachee so that they can see how they present themselves to the outside world. Alternatively, the coach may use a metaphor to illustrate or articulate the situation – an imaginative term or phrase that is used to describe an object or action. For example, using a fairground merry-go-round as a metaphor for the client's life view that they are trying to express.

Bottom lining

When a client is deep in their story, however poetic, colourful or interesting it may be, it is the responsibility of the coach to know when to say, 'Hold on a moment. What are you really trying to get at? Can you bottom line that for me?' Bottom lining is about giving the essence of the story, the strapline of the situation, the simple straightforward focus. If a client is unable to do this, then the coach needs to find out what is going on at that precise time in the coaching situation. What is being hidden? The coach also has to know and gauge when the story telling is part of the client's personal style or when it is being used as a form of resistance.

If a client is unable to bottom line a thought then it may be that they need to find clarity in the information they are expressing. At all times, the coach should be able to have a clear understanding of what is going on in the coaching process. Sometimes being honest and just asking the question, 'Hold on a moment, I'm not quite sure I understand what you're trying to say' gives the client an indication that there are discrepancies or oddities in the coaching session that need to be examined more closely.

There are other times when the client needs clarification from the coach. It may be that the coach needs to highlight a recurring pattern of behaviour or an insight and intuition. Sometimes, these truths can be shocking and difficult for the client to absorb. The client will need clarity from the coach that is helpful, insightful, caring and in the long-run deepens their client's learning and development. Above all, a client needs to be able to bottom line to get to the core of what is important and to be able to communicate that successfully.

Humour and lightness

Some of the greatest learning comes from humour. Coaching doesn't have to be a tough, serious, worthy, unrelenting process. Coaching is about learning, action and development and ways in which to gain the best from one's experiences. During the coaching process, coach and coachee will need to examine different situations, however difficult. If humour and lightness can help this process, the coach needs to be able to create it. Humour can increase the opportunities of true learning and take away the negative hammer of failure and lack of competence.

Of course, humour needs to be applied by the coach at appropriate moments. When there are sad and difficult times the client does not need to have their coach trivialising the seriousness with silly jokes. The coach needs to be sensitive to the client's need and gauge their ability to interact with a degree of lightness. Creating humour and lightness is part of having a meaningful language – and the basis of many terms and phrases that the coach and coachee may develop through the coaching relationship.

Acknowledging and championing

We all know how good it feels when some one we trust tells us how well we have done, or reminds us of the power and benefit our talents and skills give to others. In cases like this we are being acknowledged and our efforts are being championed.

The *Co-Active Coaching* model (Whitworth *et al.* 1988) has high-lighted the importance of acknowledging and championing clients as a skill. A coach needs to know how to acknowledge a client in their process of learning, taking action and developing within the coaching environment. A coach may acknowledge the client has made a recent effort to change a behaviour or learn a new skill, however successful they have been. Championing is about acknowledging a client's effort and energy to accomplish their aim.

For example, Anne needed acknowledgement she was worried about giving a presentation to peers in her industry. Anne's coach reminded her the feedback forms from previous occasions had recorded that Anne always gave the most interactive and enjoyable presentations. The coach was acknowledging her client's skills and talents and re-calling the feedback that Anne had received in the past. This gave Anne confidence and reminded her not to feel subject to any gremlin thoughts (page 98).

Championing enables a coach to bring to their client's attention what they are capable of and how this will benefit others. It is a much stronger version of acknowledging. In Anne's case, the coach went further and championed Anne by highlighting that however well the delivery of the course went, she would bring energy, passion, insight and learning to the delegates making a difficult subject enjoyable. The coach reminded Anne again that she always gave the most interactive and enjoyable presentations. The main point that Anne needed to remember was to be herself, share her experiences and not worry about delivering a perfect presentation.

5. Learning and experience

Fig. 13.   Coaching skill 5 – Learning and experience.

A mass of insights, discoveries and planned actions come out of the coaching process. These need to be learned from and experienced in order to benefit from the coaching process and develop the goals planned for future living. The skills needed to achieve this are:

♦ Perspectives and choices

♦ Re-framing

♦ Requesting and challenging

♦ Structures

♦ Re-calibrating.

Perspectives and choices

Many clients come to coaching specifically to gain new perspectives and to create choices in their lives. The skill for the coach is to be able to inspire the client to generate new perspectives and create choices that they already hold but may not be aware of. Clients are naturally creative and resourceful, but the coach still needs the skills to help them reveal these hidden perspectives and unvoiced choices especially during the peaks and plateaus of coaching.

Many times, clients gain new perspectives and choices through questioning skills such as brainstorming, inquiry and powerful questioning. Some clients come to recognise choices through the use of movement and visual tools. For example, by being asked to draw a circle on a piece of paper and dividing it into sections. The first segment in the circle can be labelled 'Don't know' and the coaching can be based around what the client doesn't know. To generate more ideas the coach could then ask 'What do you know?' and this information could be noted in the opposite segment of the circle. Another option is to ask the coachee to take a birds eye view of their situation, meta or helicopter view.

This process helps to stimulate further ideas, build on the clients new insights and create more choices, learning and self-awareness for the client. They gain greater perspective.

Creating perspectives and choices shouldn't be hampered by the fact that a coachee feels they have to accept or agree with the ideas that are being generated. Instead, it is about discovering more about a client's original thoughts and testing them out. Decision-making is the final action of this exercise.

Another exercise for clients who prefer to use movement in the coaching session is to ask the client to put an object in front of them, perhaps on their desk or on the floor. This can be done more easily if the coachee has a hands-free telephone, but is simplest to achieve if meeting the coach face to face. The coachee is asked to think of the object as a metaphor to illustrate their current considerations.

It is best if a three-dimensional object is used. For example, a coach dropped her bag in the middle of the room, letting some of the contents spill out and the bag to land in an awkward shape. She asked her client to view the options and decisions needed to take his sabbatical leave, using the metaphor of the bag sitting between them. What would the spilled items represent?

In this case, the client immediately thought of the office politics and Chinese whispers involved around who would be his temporary replacement. The coach asked 'What is needed to be able to place the items, back in the bag and close it safely?' The sagging position of the bag was also likened to the personnel management and administration chaos at home to arrange the leave details. The coach asked 'What do you need to do, and be, in order to bring this chaos back to order?'

Using a metaphor encourages a client to be objective and innovative in their actions. The object or metaphor used in each case is dependent on the learning style, and situation of the client. It doesn't necessarily have to make sense to anyone else – just the client, the coach and the confines of the coaching relationship.

Re-framing

The skill of re-framing is for the coach to help the client to consider their language and thought processes in a different way. This can be by creating more perspective and choices as described above. For example, if a client is feeling hard done by in a particular situation the coach might like to highlight that the client is thinking about the situation from a limited standpoint. The standpoint in this case is that life is like a glass half empty. The coach needs to ask their client to view the same situation from the opposite standpoint and can ask a powerful question – 'What would the situation be like if you were grateful for what you have now?' Alternatively, they could articulate where they see the client now – 'I understand that you are concerned about taking on the new tasks as part of your role, but rather than thinking of it as extra work, what if the new learning gives you the skills for the promotion you hope for?'

Requesting and challenging

Often, an obvious course of action can get pushed to the back of our minds for later attention. We experience these things in our everyday life, such as keeping accounts up to date, clearing out the garage, tidying the cupboard that throws objects out each time the doors are open. Requesting and challenging might be necessary when a client highlights the action in a longwinded manner. 'I really must clear out my old filing cabinet but I never seem to get to it. It's such a boring task and the sunshine is too good to miss at the moment. I always think of it as a winter evening's job, but I've been saying that for at least two years'. This is a good occasion for the coach to cut through the procrastination and make a simple, straightforward request.

'I request that you sort out the old filing and move the cabinet out by our next coaching session'

When a coach is making a request in this way they are asking their client to achieve something that the coach sees is important to the client. Requesting usually encourages the client to focus on an action and to carry it out. By requesting some actions the coach is asking commitment from the client to achieve them.

The client may decide that they can't do this. It could be that they feel they don't have the time or it could be that they are anxious about discovering what they have neglected to deal with. Whatever the reason the client can say 'no' or make a counter offer. For example, the coachee may say they will start the task, report progress in the next session, but agree to finish it by the end of the month. If the client says 'No', the coach needs to find out more about the reasons behind this rejection.

Challenging
Requesting can be seen in conjunction with 'challenging' – a powerful extension to requesting. Sometimes challenging is referred to as a 'mega request'. For example, Claire says she needs to generate more income soon. To achieve this Claire needs to cold call possible contacts and follow up on leads but she says that she's not good at doing it and finds that other projects always take priority. Her coach decides that since the situation is urgent and Claire would be challenged by the task, she would challenge her to contact 20 business leads and make 20 cold calls by the next session.

The idea of a challenge is that the coach chooses something that they know the client will feel is way beyond them, a real stretch. Again, the client has a choice of saying 'Yes', 'No' or counter offer. If the client says 'Yes' meekly to the coaches challenge the coach will want to check that it is really a challenge to the client – do they need a bigger challenge – or whether the client is simply stunned and will just say yes for something to say. If the answer is 'No', then the coach needs to ask, 'What would be a challenge for you in this situation / at the moment?' If the client chooses to counter offer the coach needs to know that the offer is still a challenge for the client.

The idea of a challenge is that it gets the client to do something beyond what they would have volunteered freely to do themselves. For example, if the coach asks the client 'How many business contacts will you make before our next session?' the client might venture a commitment to contacting five people. However, if the coach challenges by saying, 'I challenge you to contact 20 business leads before our next session' this challenge stretches the boundaries or possibilities for the client. Even if the coachee's counter offer is to only contact ten business leads before the next session, that is five more leads than they would have willingly volunteered to contact themselves. Challenging helps a client to build their confidence and to realise the scope of their potential.

Structures
Structures are the ways in which the client and coach have agreed to keep the client's action and learning on track. For example, the coach may request the client to keep a journal throughout the coaching process as a structure to gain insights and learning from the process. Alternatively, structures may involve a process of 'checking in' – if a client needs to make a difficult phone call the coach may request that the client contact them before making the call and after.

Other structures can include visual aids like photographs, postcards or collages that have a specific meaning to the client. Some clients who are prompted more easily by auditory structures might prefer to use aids such as alarm setting or pre-timed music to be played. These can all be good structures to remind a client to either do something on a regular basis or to remind them of an attitude of mind that they need to hold to improve their situation. Discovering what structures suit the client best is a key factor in founding the coaching relationship.

Re-calibrating
During the process of learning and being to able to review current experiences, the fourth stage of the learning process (see Chapter 4) is to re-calibrate actions and attitudes that are needed to achieve more positive outcomes.

Just as a coach helps a client to re-frame their thoughts and perspectives, so a coach can also help their client to gain more perspective and choices by being able to assess and if necessary re-calibrate actions for the future. Many clients that request coaching are perfectionists and high achievers. Perfectionism is the endless loop of indecision and a coach needs to give their client the confidence to take action to move forward irrespective of whether the outcome will be perfect.

Most learning comes from experience, and in many cases experience may have to have been the result of failure. Failure – which is often regarded as a negative experience – can actually help to achieve the desired result by re-calibrating actions and processes. The coach will need to point out that all experience is instructive and gives information whether good or bad – this experience provides the 'compost' for future learning and achievement.

THE COACH'S OWN TRAINING AND DEVELOPMENT

People come to coaching via many different routes, experiences and levels of knowledge. There are increasing numbers of coaching models and training courses available. As a result, deciding how to continue with ongoing professional development and to qualify for membership of professional coaching bodies can be a confusing process.

There are many different routes to train as a coach and continue with professional development. The three main ways that people have previously experienced coaching skill training are:

1) In-house company training – coaching skills for managers
2) Voluntary sector training – coaching and mentoring skills
3) Adult learning classes – often as a module in professional or personal qualifications.

To help finding further training and development contact details of professional coaching bodies can be found in the Resources Section (see page 186). These coaching bodies recommend training that they consider to be acceptable to their ethics and standards and offer a high level of ongoing continuous professional development (CPD).

Professional coaches need to be coached using an ongoing coaching relationship with a coach. A famous proverb says 'Don't eat in a restaurant run by a thin chef'. In the same way clients do not trust the coaching relationship with a coach who is not actively being coached. Over time, coaches benefit from working with different coaches. Some coaches will act as mentors for business and continual professional development, while others will have been chosen to support more personal areas of life. By being coached themselves, coaches will be able to experience the full range of coaching interactions and training skills that will enable them to feel, understand and benefit from a range of different coaching styles.

A coach's own coaching experiences will give insights into how it feels to be coached, and an understanding as to what makes a coaching sessions and the coaching relationship truly valuable. With this knowledge a coach will have a clearer understanding of what kind of coach they wish to be, who they would like as clients and what their clients will be involved in throughout their coaching commitment. The experience will help a coach to answer the following questions:

♦ What does it feel like to have a moment when 'the light bulb is switched on'?

♦ How do you react to questions that feel risky and too penetrating for you?

♦ What do you physically experience when you are feeling resistant in a session?

♦ How do you like silence in a coaching session?

♦ What makes you trust your coach?

♦ How are you gaining insights?

♦ What did the coach 'do' and how did they have to 'be' to create the best coaching environment?

♦ What information did you ask for from your coach before deciding to work with them?

COACHING HOMEWORK

What insights did you have while answering the above questions?

What do you need to develop to further your existing skills?

SUPERVISION FOR COACHES

Part of a coach's training and ongoing professional development is to work with a coach mentor who will coach and mentor their development. A coach mentor offers their experience and expertise of working in the coaching profession and can therefore act as a mentor for the trainee coach as well as working with them in a coaching relationship.

A coach mentor will work with their client to help improve their coaching business but also to coach them on personal areas of their life. Part of this role is to be available to discuss any problems, insights or issues that the trainee coach may have with their own clients. It is also becoming increasingly common for coach mentors to supervise a coach in their techniques, dynamics and relationships with their clients. Coaching supervision models have been adapted from supervision models used in the caring professions to cover three main points of view that exist in the coaching sessions. The supervisor is concerned with:

1) Reflecting on the coaching session itself and the content.
2) Understanding the coach's interaction and dynamics of the coaching relationship.
3) Reviewing the coaching session and the development of the coach during the supervised session.

COACHING HOMEWORK

Either tape a coaching session to review later, or answer these questions immediately after coaching while the interaction is still fresh in your mind. Ask your client to give you feedback on their experiences of the session. What was beneficial for them? What would they like more or less of? How do they feel at the end of the session? What did they feel you missed? What mark would they give you for the session 1–10 (10 being the highest).

SELF-ASSESSMENT OF THE COACHING SESSION

◆ How did I as a coach experience the coaching session?

◆ What did I experience physically and emotionally during the session?

◆ How did the coachee experience the session? Include the answers from their feedback.

◆ What happened between me and my coachee? Positive and negative results.

◆ What skills did I use during the session?

◆ What skills would have been more beneficial to use?

◆ How do I rate my performance as a coach 1–10 (10 being the highest mark).

Regular use of the self-assessment of coaching is a useful tool to help coaches focus on the impact and development of their coaching.

SELF-MANAGEMENT FOR THE COACH

There are two sides that make up self-development for the coach. They are:

1) As a professional coach
2) As personal self-care.

Self-management as the professional coach

Self-management is a form of balance that the coach needs to master and to exercise at all times within the coaching relationship. On the one hand the coach needs to stand back and allow their clients to create insight, learning, action and experience for themselves. On the other hand, the coach needs to be fully present in the relationship – to challenge rather than to collude and to be observant in listening and seeing what is said and unsaid in the relationship. It is not a coach's job to be directive or give advice. That is the role of a consultant. The coach's role is to highlight discrepancies in actions, assumptions or attitudes; hold the coachee's agenda; provide a safe and courageous coaching environment; and use tools to add different perspectives, choices, learning and experience for the client.

There are eight skills that have been identified as critical for the coach to master in order to be self-managed in relation to their clients. These are:

1) **Compassion** – an understanding of people's difficulties, dilemmas and suffering
2) **Non-judgemental** – setting aside criteria of judgement relating to people and situations
3) **Boundaries** – know the healthy, life-giving limits to self, relationships and culture
4) **Signposting other resources** – keeping clients' best interests central, not the coaches
5) **Unattached to outcomes** – not controlling the end result
6) **Hold the focus** – allowing exploration of the agenda, but not losing end focus
7) **Value difference and diversity** – opening up all avenues and welcoming innovation
8) **Aware of own intuitiveness** – to create new possibilities and insight.

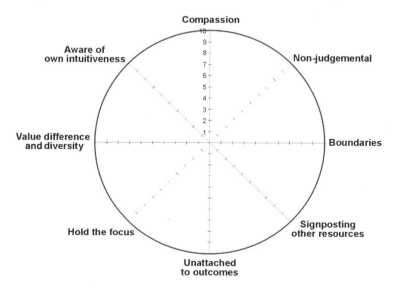

Fig. 14.   Wheel of self-management skills.

Self-management as personal self-care

Self-management also includes the self-care of the coach themself. Coaches are not expected to be perfect people leading perfectly ordered lives, but they do need to practice and aim for a balanced, fulfilled and purposeful life. That way they will be able to give their clients the highest level of coaching professionalism.

COACHING HOMEWORK

Complete the check of self management skills in Figure 14.

Review these skills and rate your aptitude to these skills 1–10 (10 being the highest).

What skills do you need to develop?

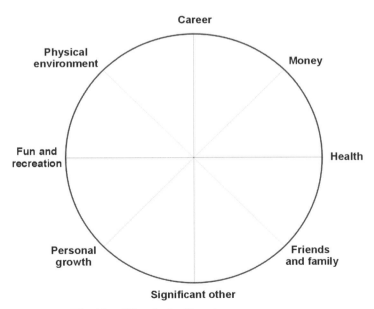

Fig. 15.   Wheel of self-caring management.

COACHING HOMEWORK

To identify your own levels of self-caring management, complete the exercise of the Wheel of Life to help to sustain a balanced, purposeful life for you as a coach (for further development see Chapter 3 and Figure 18).

What areas of your personal life do you need to develop, change or re-calibrate?

IN SUMMARY

In order to prepare yourself to be an effective coach you will need to:

♦   Recognise personal qualities

♦   Audit existing competencies and skills

♦   Identify areas of coaching training and development needed

♦   Assess self-management

♦   Ensure a fulfilled, balanced and purposeful life for yourself

2
Building the Coaching Relationship and Managing Client's Expectations

In any relationship, there is usually some degree of expectation that either fuels the relationship or quashes it. The coaching relationship is unusual on many levels. It is designed to be free from the demands of normal friend, family and workplace agendas and expectations. The power of a coaching relationship is that the energy, commitment and experiences are all directed to aid the client's agenda, aims and objectives, rather than the coach's own agenda or personality.

The nature of this unconditional, giving and supportive relationship is sometimes difficult for clients to truly appreciate and trust in the beginning. Particularly in third party or sponsored-coaching scenarios. Coaches fundamentally wish the best for their clients – whatever that looks like at the end of the coaching process. Within the coaching process, the coach uses their skills and expertise to support the client's agenda, broader purpose and process of action, experience and learning.

MANAGING EXPECTATIONS

Over time a coaching mantra has emerged that 'the coach has no agenda – except to be able to facilitate the client's agenda'. This is statement is true up to a point. However, a coaching relationship is based on a professional interaction and therefore, it is only natural that the coach

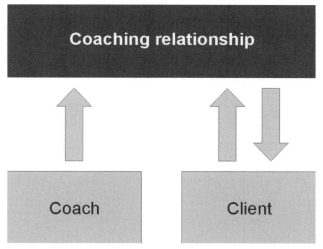

Fig. 16. The interaction and flow of the coaching relationship energies.

has some expectations of their clients. They expect their clients to have commitment, to keep their appointments, be open and honest in all exchanges, to pay their fees on time and to have a mutual respect of the coaching relationship and process. The client also has expectations over and above having designed a coaching relationship that supports them. They expect to be working with a trained professional – who acts in a professional manner.

This chapter looks at the first step towards developing a coaching relationship – the initial contact between the coach and coachee. This first step needs to ensure that client expectations are answered in ways that establish a healthy coaching relationship for the future. The points that need to be covered for this to happen are:

◆   Finding the right coach – which is the best coach for the client and their needs?

◆   The purpose of coaching – is coaching the most beneficial way of working with the client at this time?

◆ Referring prospective clients – what policy should be taken when the initial coaching contact reveals that an ongoing relationship is not viable?

FINDING THE RIGHT COACH

Which is the best coach for the client and their needs? This is a decision that needs to be considered from:

(a) The client's wants and needs
and
(b) The coach's position as a professional.

The client's wants and needs

Many prospective clients start working with coaches not knowing fully what the relationship and process will do for them. Often the comment is that 'I don't really know what to expect – but I will give it a go'. Usually someone they respect has recommended the process to them and that is enough to broker a sense of trust. They may not be conscious of any expectations and truly believe that they are entering a relationship openly. This is rarely the reality of the situation.

There are always expectations when entering into a professional relationship. At the very least, there is an expectation of a high level of competence within all personal and organisational interactions. Therefore, even if the client is emotionally willing to trust the coach, without having a clear sense of the future outcome, this trust will be eroded if the basics of personal politeness, timeliness, ethics and standards are not present at all times.

The coach's position as a professional

All coaches need to decide what their professional ethics and standards are, and how they would like to work with their clients. This will form the terms, conditions and coaching policy used for the coaching commitment. Every coach is an individual who uses their uniqueness to create the best possible conditions for the client. However, the longer a coach practices and the differing client situations they encounter, the more likely they are to need to review their terms, conditions, ethic and standards on a regular basis. If you are setting up a business as a coach there is greater depth of discussion on this topic in Chapter 6. Each coach needs to decide on a framework that they feel is most aligned to their values and vision as a coach.

Over a period of six months, a survey of coaches and coachees revealed the top ten questions asked by a client during the initial contact with a coach. These questions are usually asked to assess the suitability of a coach.

The top 10 questions were:

1. What are your qualifications as a coach?
2. Which professional coaching body are you a member of?
3. What ethics and standards can I expect from your professional body and what do they do for me as a client?
4. What led you to being a coach?
5. Where are your coaching skills most used and with who? (answer without breaking client confidentiality)
6. What commitment do you want from me as your client? (time and regularity)
7. How do you work with your clients? (telephone, face to face, 1:1, groups)
8. What happens if 'it' doesn't work?
9. Do you have a coach?
10. I'm not exactly sure what I want to be coached on – how can you help me?

What are your answers to the above set of questions?

How will you use this information to be fully prepared to answer a prospective client's queries and expectations about the benefits of coaching for them?

What are you willing to do to help prospective clients find the right coach for them?

PERSONALITY STYLE

A selection of models are outlined below to identify different styles and personality types. Some of your clients may have been given one of these models to identify their behaviours and personalities (For example the Meyer Briggs models or systems based on DISC already in the workplace).

Psychometric testing and personality style typing are products that some coaches offer to increase income stream for their business. These are not tools and skills that are part of a coach's competencies but products in their own right. Complementary income generation is discussed further in Chapter 6. However, as a coach it is useful to have a basic understanding of personality styles, types and the differing ways of learning that clients may display. This will enable you to leverage the maximum benefit of the coaching process from your clients.

DISC

For an illustration of differing styles and personality types one of the easiest models to grasp is 'DISC'. This is a language used to describe 'how we act' or our behaviour. Research has show that characteristics can be grouped together into four styles.

D = dominance – challenge
I = influence – contacts
S = steadiness – consistency
C = compliance – constraints

> As W.M. Marston believes 'All people exhibit all four behavioural factors in varying degrees of intensity'
>> ('Emotions of Normal People' from *The Universal Language DISC*. 1993 TTI Ltd.)

Phil Sandahl co-author of *Co-Active Coaching* estimates that 50 per cent of coaches come to be 'held' by the coach 'until they come alive' and the other 50 per cent come to make life changing choices. The following brief descriptions of the DISC types are shown in relation to their natural behavioral style of actions and their reactions to change in their world.

High 'Ds' – love change and will change the status quo. They will re-invent the old way, focusing on one goal – results. They 'rock the boat' in their quest for results and will find more efficient ways to get the job done. Their high emotion is anger/short fuse.

High 'Is' – may not notice change but a natural mediator, not liking conflict. They can verbally persuade both sides to come to an agree-ment. Part of this is due to their ability to focus on the bright side of the issues. People tend to like them, and 'buy' their concepts and ideas.

High 'Ss' – don't like change and need much preparation. Once in-volved in the planning process they are a great asset. They can bring lofty ideas back into the realm of the real world and point out the gaps and flaws in the plan due to their logical thinking process.

High 'Cs' – concerned by the effects of change. They are great objective thinkers and task oriented. Their sceptical nature looks at all the possibilities before they buy into the plan. If allowed to use their natural talents, they are a great asset to a team when carrying through a plan. They collect data, and are always analysing, testing and clarifying.

Having read through these basic style types, you will see that different people work best and embrace change at different stages of the coaching process. They will also react to the process of change in contradictory ways to each other.

COACHING HOMEWORK

What is your DISC style and type?

How do you need to develop to be able to work with the other DISC types as clients?

PERSONAL WORKING STYLES

Five distinctly different working styles have been described by Julie Hay in her book *Working It Out At Work: Understanding Attitudes And Building Relationships.* Each working style expresses different drives and motivations.

The five personal working styles are:

♦ Hurry Ups

♦ Try Hards

♦ Be Strong

♦ Be Perfect

♦ Please People.

Hurry Ups

Hurry Ups, as the name suggests, like to do things efficiently and in the shortest time possible. They respond well to deadlines and pressure seems to gear up their energy. Their great strength is that they can deliver whatever they are asked to do. Non-verbal behaviour is displayed by actions such as foot and finger tapping and checking their watch. They get very distressed if they have too much time to think or if there is a silence during a conversation. They often become frustrated at planning or reflection stages of learning and experience, so a coach will need to encourage them to appreciate and benefit from these stages to achieve the best end goal.

Try Hards

Try Hards work hard and display determination and enthusiasm with projects. They love to get involved, to plan and carry out a project at the beginning but find the final stages of a task, particularly when it is going well, difficult to complete. Non-verbal behaviour includes sitting forward and having an impatient manner sometimes and clenched fists. It is important for Try Hards that the coach supports them in completing a project and celebrates their successes in order for them to understand the true value of their effort.

Be Strongs

Be Strongs are self-sufficient and task orientated. They are usually the people who stay calm while projects are falling to pieces and everyone is panicking. They find it difficult to admit weakness, they tend to take on far too much work, rather than admit that they may not be able to cope. They tend to be very self-critical and consider asking for help a weakness. Non-verbal behaviour includes immobile face and body when trying to hide any evidence of feelings, both positive or negative. They often have an aloof manner, speak in a dispassionate tone of voice and have a habit of straightening their clothes.

Be Perfect

Be Perfect, as the name suggests, strive for perfection and excellence. They like to get it right first time, they check facts and details, plan ahead and are well organised. In some ways they are the opposites of Hurry Ups who just need to complete the job as quickly as possible. Their non-verbal behaviour includes pursing of lips, controlled tone of voice, co-ordinated clothes and obsessive compulsive habits. They hate to lose control and can be seen to be very judgemental of other people's behaviours.

Please People

Please People, as the term suggests, like to please people and create harmony. They make good team members, they like to work in a consultative fashion and will accommodate others in any way that stops them from being rejected or found wanting in some way. They are often in denial of their own wants and needs to a level that can be harmful for them in reality but they would explain away as being considerate behaviour towards others. Their non-verbal behaviour includes smiling a lot, being a good listener, allowing others to interrupt them. They often blame themselves even when it is not their responsibility but underneath the smiling face there is very often a high level of stress.

Which personal working style best describes you?

What do you need to develop to work with people who have other styles?

DIFFERING LEARNING STYLES

Research shows that we each have preferred ways of learning – Honey and Mumford (1992) *Using Your Learning Styles*. The four preferred learning styles are:

♦ *Activists* feel more comfortable learning from experience. They tend to prefer activity to reflection and are rather impatient with academic debate and theories. When they buy a new gadget they are more likely to try it out, and learn by doing, than by reading the book of instructions.

♦ *Reflectors* feel more comfortable learning by listening, reading or observing. They prefer to avoid learning situations where they are required to be in the limelight.

♦ *Theorists* feel more comfortable when learning by solving problems, using analytical skills and relating what is being learnt to a broader system, model, theory or to the 'big picture'. They like ideas even if they do not have an immediate application. They are suspicious of checklists and assertions unsupported by research data.

♦ *Pragmatists* feel more comfortable acquiring knowledge and skills that have an immediate practical application. They like tips that can be put into effect. They tend to be less interested in analysis and theories. Checklists appeal to them.

Daniel Goldman's *The New Leaders* illustrates these differing learning modes in a different way based on Kolb's learning style inventory:

♦ Concrete experience (activists) – having an experience that allows them to see and feel what it is.

♦ Reflection (reflectors) – thinking about their own and others' experiences.

♦ Model building (theorists) – coming up with a theory that makes sense of what they observe.

♦ Trial and error (pragmatists) – trying something out by actively experimenting with a new approach.

COACHING HOMEWORK

Which is your preferred way to learn?

How do you accommodate the different styles of learning of your clients?

The type of questions that clients ask of their coaches give a great insight into what they are feeling. Questions express unspoken information about attitudes, values, desires and personal interactions with others. Here is a list of specific questions that have been asked by clients, during the initial coaching contact:

♦ *'I'm always travelling in different times zones – how do we arrange a regular coaching time?'*

♦ *'I hate all that 'woo woo' – close your eyes, think of the future and miracles happen stuff. How do you coach?'*

♦ *'I need to make decisions about this now – what can you do for me now?'*

♦ *'I don't know what I want – but a friend said it helped her. What do I have to do?'*

♦ *'I, er . . . Um . . . I er . . . think I need to find a new job. Um . . . I . . .* (Coach recorded 10 second pause) *don't think . . . my boss will keep me . . . on . . . with the changes . . .* (long pause) *at work. Do you help other people with this?'*

♦ *'My mother recently died and I can't seem to get on with the business of winding up the estate, dealing with my family – I'm the only family executive – and I've my own life to deal with. That feels a mess right now. Can you help and advise me?'*

COACHING HOMEWORK

What do you think are the expectations of the clients asking these questions?

How will you manage these expectations?

What sense of differing styles, learning and personality types do you gain from these client questions?

These questions lead on to the next level of consideration – is coaching what your client needs?

THE PURPOSE OF COACHING

Is coaching the most beneficial way of working with the client at this time?

In the initial stages of the coaching process a coach has the opportunity to get to know the needs and expectations of their client, and to discover if coaching is right for their needs.

The case of two clients
Veronique and Mary both wanted help to establish a new direction in their careers and had been referred to coaching by friends.

During the initial telephone conversation the coach asked two key questions:

♦ What would a different job need to give you that you don't already have in your current occupation?

♦ What made you decide to ask for a coach's support at this time?

These questions are good examples of powerful and open questions that allowed prospective clients to respond in a truthful and meaningful way.

Veronique's story
Veronique's answers highlighted the fact that Veronique had often quarrelled with her partner about their future, careers and permanent home. They had both come to the UK because of their work. Veronique said she had sought medical help for stress and that her partner admitted he felt strained too. He also recognised he regularly lost his temper. He had agreed that they needed support to decide the next way forward. He was also willing for her to do the research and arrange for him to seek any help necessary, including help for his feelings of anger and frustration. The reason Veronique was calling at this time was because she and her partner had had a violent argument the night before.

It was clear to the coach that there were issues with Veronique and her partner's relationship that overshadowed Veronique's desire to change direction in career. Before coaching could be of real benefit, the coach felt that there was a need for therapy as a couple to tackle their joint commitment of a future together and the dynamics within their relationship. The coach was able to identify and discuss these sensitive issues with Veronique, refer her to relationship therapist and encourage her to ask her own doctor for further referrals. Veronique returned to coaching nine months later.

Mary's story

In Mary's case, the questions highlighted the fact that Mary had given up working to be with her children three years earlier. She had not found this transition of roles from 'city career Mum' to 'at home Mum' to be as easy as she thought. Although she did not earn a salary at this time, she had contributed to the family assets by developing and moving the family into their new home. Now she was ready for a new challenge that interested her, allowed her time with the family and gave her the ability to earn her own money for the fun things she wanted for herself and the family.

The coach was happy to support Mary to find a new direction for a career. Mary was now settled in her role and relationships. She appreciated the time she was having with her children but realised that, because they were growing up, she now had more time to do things for herself. Mary and her husband loved travelling and an extra income would make this more feasible. This time, however, she wanted to really enjoy how she earned her income and have control over her working hours to fit in with family life.

Checklist for coach:

♦ Are you happy to coach this person?

♦ Do you feel professionally that you can support their needs, expectations and goals?

♦ Are there issues being discussed that you feel uncomfortable with?

♦ What makes you want to enter into a coaching relationship with this client?

If you and your prospective client are happy to move forward to the next step of the coaching relationship, you will need to agree with them:

(a) Logistics and fees for coaching
(b) Terms and conditions to commence a coaching contract
(c) Date and venue for the next coaching session
(d) Where to send any information or preparatory 'welcome' pack.

REFERRING PROSPECTIVE CLIENTS

What is the best policy for a coach when an ongoing relationship is not viable?

If the initial coaching conduct reveals that the coaching relationship will not be taken further, the coach needs to conclude the relationship and act as a referral to further the client's agenda.

When giving any professional referrals it is essential that the clients know that neither the coach nor the professionals involved are in any way colluding or benefiting in an unprofessional manner. Each referral must be based on the client's agenda and needs and not for the benefit of the referrer. Any information given is done so with the client taking full responsibility to undertake their own due diligence of the services and products offered before entering into any contract or making any payments.

BARRIERS TO LEARNING AND EXPERIENCE

It is worth taking time to understand some of the barriers that might get in the way of a coachee's learning and willingness to experience further development.

Common barriers to learning are:

♦   Previous experience

♦   Fear of failure/success

♦   Fear of change

♦   Lack of motivation

♦   Lack of confidence

♦   Too old to learn.

Previous experience

All clients come with a history of experience, failure, success and attitudes to learning. This may overshadow their willingness to discover differing perspectives, trying new ways of doing things, and generally make them wary of taking certain steps forward. It is important that the coach and the coachee are totally honest in discussing the effects of previous experiences that may affect future learning and development. By gaining insights into the negative effects of previous experience, the client finds the courage to continue to willingly take steps forward.

Fear of failure/success

For some people (such as a perfectionist) fear of failure is a great barrier to going through a process of experimentation and learning. However, other people, (such as a people pleaser) find the idea of success a frightening state. It exposes them and holds them up for possible ridicule and criticism. A coach needs to understand and be willing to highlight any clues that are presented by the client that illustrate a barrier to the coaching process in these ways.

Fear of change

In spite of the fact that change is constantly happening on a daily basis in our lives, for many people the idea of change taking place from a state of intention and consciousness is frightening. For many people it is much easier to react to change than it is to be proactive. There is a need for the coach to illustrate, in a non-judgemental way, any indications they see of this fear of change having a negative effect on the client's current life or in some way having an adverse effect on their future vision and agenda in the coaching process.

Lack of motivation

If the coachee is not truly behind the actions needed to achieve their goals and agenda then the chances of success are small. When clients repeatedly state that they wish to do 'something' and yet consistently never get round to it, or create situations that make achievement impossible, it is a good sign to a coach that the client is not compelled to achieve this aim. The coach needs to highlight this and support the client in finding out what the real agenda is and why they have been clouding the issues with goals they have no genuine interest in.

Lack of confidence

The label 'lack of confidence' has become a blanket phrase. If a client says they lack confidence for a particular element of learning and development, the coach needs to discover why confidence is lacking in this case and not generally throughout their life. The question 'What is it about this issue that makes you feel like . . . a six year old girl/a wobbly jelly' will give insight to the coachee of the levels of confidence they have through their life. In some cases a lack of confidence isn't creating the barrier to learning – rather it is a guise for other reasons like fear of failure or fear of success.

Too old to learn

It's amazing – whatever the age of the client – how often a coach hears the words 'I'm too old to learn that now'. The proverb 'You can't teach an old dog new tricks' is another guise, usually for some other barrier to learning. It may be that the coachee has been brought up to believe that there is a right time to do everything and once you have missed that time you have missed the opportunity. For example, a client who had left school failing to gain entrance to university may feel that they are not good enough to go to university. Luckily today, if you want to become a mature student there are no barriers for you choosing to do it at any stage of life. If a client feels that they are too old, it may also be that they are frightened of going back to study, trying to use skills that have lain dormant for the last twenty-five years and that they may not be the perfect student.

Going back to studying often means that clients feel they are exposing themselves to criticism. If they have had bad experiences in the past, they may also feel vulnerable to the 'establishment' (such as the teacher) as if they have returned back to school. Some clients feel as though they will lose control and power in their own development.

SEEKING ADDITIONAL HELP

The coach will need to decide if these are barriers that can be worked through in the coaching process or if they indicate a much deeper issue or fear that requires a different kind of expertise. Coaches, whether working in their own practice or internally in the workplace, are encouraged to gather and collate their own professional contacts and resource lists (for more details see the coaches toolkit listed in Chapter 6). This will enable the coach to serve the client's agenda and needs in the best way possible when concluding the coaching relationship at this stage.

Sometimes, after the initial contact between a coachee and client, it is decided not to continue the relationship. It could be that the client has issues that would not benefit from coaching and they need to be signposted to other services (see list of Resources on page 186). It may be that both the client and the coach simply do not 'gel'. In which case it would be helpful if the coach had a list of other coaches to whom they could refer them. Many coaches have decided as a business policy to either specialise or create a niche of coaching which may be more appropriate to a prospective client's needs. On the other hand it could be a case that the coach feels they would rather not coach this particular client for some professional boundaries or values that they hold.

PUTTING THINGS ON HOLD

In the case history illustrated by Veronique's story, there are times when coaching is not right for the client. This does not mean that coaching will not be suitable in the future. It may be that the client needs to work through some issues that overshadow the client's goals in the future. It is up to a coach to be able to discuss these issues sensitively with a client and help them to clarify what the immediate next steps are. In the case of Veronique, having been referred to another professional and back to her doctor, it was agreed that she would call the coach at an appointed time in the month ahead to check in with the coach on her progress. During this check-in call the client asked if she could book a second check-in telephone call with the coach in six months' time to discuss her progress.

Nine months after Veronique's initial contact with the coach she started the coaching process. The coach was happy to accommodate her, even though during this time the client was not yet paying coaching fees. The coach felt it was part of their professional values to be able to support Veronique in this way, which led to a full coaching relationship nine months after the initial contact. Veronique had valued her coach's honesty from the beginning, trusted the level of support given throughout and appreciated the agreement that had been fulfilled.

PUTTING CLIENTS IN THE PICTURE

It is the responsibility of the coach to be truthful and to point out any discrepancies or oddities that they hear during their conversation with prospective clients. At all times they must be sensitive to their client's wants and needs. There are some coaches who make a policy of always asking how many other coaches the prospective client has approached. These coaches insist that any prospective client speaks to at least three coaches to discuss differing coaching styles, terms, conditions and fees.

There are also coaches who offer free introductory coaching sessions for half an hour so that the prospective client can get a feel of the coaching process. There is much current debate within the coaching community as to how informative a free coaching session is for a client. Some coaches are aware of prospective clients making numerous free introductory appointments with coaches as a way of trying to get free coaching or 'just in time' coaching on immediate issues or situations that they have.

Whatever your decision about taking on a prospective client you will need to conclude an introductory session in a professional manner. To prepare for the second stage of creating the coaching relationship it can be helpful for the coachee to complete a simple questionnaire. Here is an example of a simple, but informative questionnaire that a coach can use in the initial contact session.

(1) What three things would you like most to get out of coaching in the first three months? Be as specific as you can.

(2) Where in your life do you feel the most stuck at the moment?

(3) What are your real strengths?

(4) The most important thing in your life is . . . (please complete)

(5) The thing/area I would most like to get rid of is . . . (please complete)

(6) Please create a list of items you have been procrastinating about and are ready to handle now.

(7) Please send your life story in any form that works for you best.

SUMMARY

At the first stage of building a coaching relationship and managing clients' expectations the coach needs to ensure:

♦ The client and coach need to be the right match for each other.

♦ That coaching is right for the client at this time and for their wants and needs

♦ The coach must be prepared to refer clients to other professionals where appropriate.

♦ Any referrals must be made without benefit to, or influence by, the coach's needs.

♦ The client's wants and needs are paramount.

3
Creating the Foundation of the Coaching Relationship

This stage is the second step in building a coaching relationship. It moves the relationship forward to the firm commitment of creating a foundation from which the coaching relationship will spring into the ongoing coaching process (see Figure 1). It is referred to here in *Learning to Coach* as the 'springboard' session, creating is the first key phase of the coaching process (see Figure 7).

DIFFERENT COACHING STYLES

Coaches manage the foundation of the coaching relationship in different ways, depending on their personal coaching styles. Coaches' preferences and styles range from a 'welcome' pack or a simple list of questions for the coachee to answer in preparation for the ongoing coaching session (as shown in Chapter 2), to arranging a two-day 'breakout session' with the client and coach in a neutral place, perhaps even roughing it in the countryside. However a coach chooses to organise the foundation session, they need to be sensitive to their client's needs. An overloaded, time pressured individual may not appreciate a 'welcome' pack to be completed and returned before the coaching session. The coach needs to know how to accommodate a client's needs. Some coaches decide to set a framework of working and leave it up to a potential client to decide if they wish to be coached within that structure.

Other coaches offer a range of options with which to create and build the springboard session depending on their client's needs. For example, a global executive may find that two days away is easier to arrange and gives them the opportunity to tune out the distractions and demands of work and life to concentrate, reflect, clarify and plan for the ongoing coaching sessions. On the other hand, a busy working mum with young children may prefer to hold the springboard session during the first month's weekly coaching sessions. This, for her, is the least disruptive and stressful way to accommodate her family and work commitments.

However the coach and coachee decides to arrange the springboard session, setting up the foundation of a coaching relationship ensures the maximum benefits, insights and results from the coaching process.

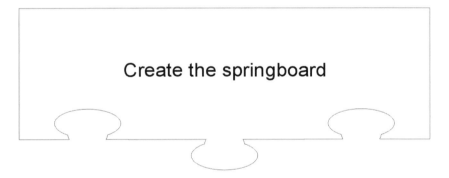

Create the springboard

Fig. 17. Creating the springboard – 1st key phase of coaching process.

GETTING TO KNOW YOUR CLIENT

The purpose of this springboard session is to gather information that allows the coach and the coachee to discover where the client is now and how that influences their decisions. It includes the discovery of a client's governing values, attitudes, purpose in life, understanding of the world around them, levels of engagement and how different choices affect their experiences. Together the coach and coachee will clarify and define the aims and objectives of the coaching relationship and any means of measurement needed to track the progress for themselves and/or the organisation sponsoring the coaching programme.

In this session the coach and client may review the logistics and working alliance they originally agreed in the initial contact stage, and any other factors that could make the relationship succeed or be less than valuable for the client. In addition, they may discuss the boundaries of confidentiality, the responsibilities of both the coach and coachee to the ongoing coaching relationship and what would make the coaching environment safe, courageous and productive for the client.

SETTING OBJECTIVES

Having established the realities of the present, there is also a need to clarify and define the objectives of the coaching relationship and the future values, vision and agenda of the client.

This is the case whether the coaching is described as executive coaching, life coaching or any other niche label of coaching specialities. However the springboard session is conducted, it needs to be in a way that is intentionally created and worked through to maximise the ongoing opportunities and benefits of the coaching process. Starting a long-term coaching relationship without a solid understanding of the client and their needs is like building a house without a solid foundation – possible, but shaky and liable to fall down.

This chapter will cover:

♦ what makes a safe and courageous coaching space

♦ the co-designing and logistics of a coaching relationship

♦ the five viewpoints of future life – VALUE

◆ the goals and primary focus of coaching

◆ the responsibility of the coach and coachee.

Examples of blank forms to record these sessions are found in the Coaches toolkit (see Chapter 6). When completed, these create a record of the information for both the client and the coach which they can refer back to during the coaching sessions.

SAFE AND COURAGEOUS COACHING SPACE

The three elements that make a safe and courageous coaching space are:

◆ Trust

◆ Confidentiality

◆ Non-judgement.

The coaching process can either be face to face or on the telephone, but in both cases a safe and courageous coaching 'space' is created. If you are coaching face to face the coach and coachee meet in a physical environment. This needs to be quiet and contained to encourage learning and experimentation within the session. However, even if the coaching session takes place over the telephone, a coaching 'space' can be created, although it is an intangible 'place'. Again, both the client and coach need to be in a quiet space where they cannot be overheard. For both parties, a hands free telephone set enables more freedom of movement during the call.

Trust and confidentiality

A safe and courageous coaching space is created by the coachee knowing that: 1) whatever is said and takes place within the coaching conversation is totally confidential; 2) the coachee has come to trust that whatever subjects the coach broaches and whatever they are requested to do, the client knows that it is in the service of their own agenda and coaching goals; 3) that this coaching space is somewhere that the client can be totally honest and truthful with themselves and the coach.

Non-judgement

This 'space' is also a forum in which the client can practice new behaviour, explore new experiences and be totally open and honest about feelings and intellectual analysis, knowing that the coach is committed to being non-judgemental and totally respecting of the difference and diversity of their client.

Setting the scene

The physical environment is important for both face-to-face and telephone coaching sessions. A face-to-face coaching session works best when the location is a neutral space for the client, i.e. not in their home or office. Some coaches are members of institutions and clubs that have quiet corners or hire out rooms on an hourly basis. Other coaches arrange to meet their clients in hotel lounges where they can comfortably conduct the coaching session without being overheard and have light refreshments served. Some coaches stipulate that neither they nor their clients will drink alcoholic beverages during the coaching session. Other coaches have decided that they never conduct a coaching session during a meal. Coaches whose style is very physically mobile, might make the decision to only to conduct their face to face coaching sessions in a private room or in their own office.

A telephone coaching session works best if the client calls their coach from a telephone in a quiet room where they will not be overheard or interrupted by others and there is no ambient background noise. The same applies for email and other technological media used for the coaching session. It is very possible that during the call the coach can request that the client physically moves. In Chapter 1 we discussed the concept of 'coaching geography' and we will discuss the practical application during the coaching process more fully in Chapter 4.

Keeping the boundaries

It is important to point out at this stage that there may be clients that think it is good time management to conduct their coaching session while doing something else. For example, making a telephone session while driving their car home at the end of the day or arranging that the weekly telephone coaching call would efficiently take place while they were preparing the special 'once a week' family get together dinner. This may be due to time pressures or simply down to their personalities.

Coaches need to be assertive about the boundaries they decide to use within their coaching sessions. Clients can forget that a coaching session is not merely a helpful, encouraging and supportive conversation. If a coaching session is conducted in a relaxed atmosphere a coachee can underestimate the high level of physical and mental activity involved. Coaching involves a lot of left and right brain activity and a client needs to give a hundred per cent of their concentration, awareness and thought processes to each session. The automatic responses of driving a car, preparing dinner for the family or any other multi-tasking actions will not allow the client to be fully cognitive and present.

Breaking confidentiality

Although ensuring total confidentiality is one of the ways in which the safe and courageous coaching is achieved there can be rare occasions when a coach may have to consider breaking confidentiality. In some cases they may be legally required to do so, such as in the violent treatment of children. In one case a coach found that they were having a telephone call with a newly referred client who was in a very fragile state of mind. The coach felt duty bound to contact other professionals, including the person who had referred the new client in order to find family and friends to contact and alert them to the situation. In this case the parents were contacted and their child was admitted to hospital with a suspected overdose. It is to be stressed, this is not a normal occurrence for coaches – however coaches have to be prepared to act according to their professional responsibility.

It could be that a client knows about regular theft from their employer or repeatedly takes time off work themselves to recover from action-packed weekends. Their explanation is that 'duvet days' are an acceptable employee right in the 21st century. It is not the place of the coach to be judgemental about what is going on, but rather to highlight the unease that they have with the situation. Once these actions are expressed honestly between the coach and coachee they can be addressed. The client may need the support of their coach in order to deal with these issues. If the client chooses to ignore their advice, the coach is duty bound to tell the coachee how (legally or professionally) they are obliged to deal with them. This is not a step to be taken lightly – and should be one of the areas that is addressed in the ethic and standards of each coach (see Chapter 6).

CO-DESIGNING AND LOGISTICS OF THE COACHING RELATIONSHIP

From the initial contact, the coach and client will have discussed the basic practicalities of the coaching relationship. These include:

- Mode of coaching – telephone or face to face

- Location and coaching contact details for each session

- Frequency of sessions

- Length of coaching session

- Level of ongoing coaching support between appointments

- Length of coaching commitment

- Level of coaching aftercare beyond the closure of relationship

- Coaching fees

- Terms and conditions of coaching contract

- Any special conditions needed for the coaching relationship.

These practicalities need to be reviewed and confirmed in the springboard session. Any further expectations the client has of the process also need to be highlighted at this stage.

Moving forward

Sometimes the springboard session illuminates concerns that are not coaching issues or highlights areas and loose ends that need to be dealt with before a valuable coaching relationship and process can begin to move forward.

For example, one new client needed to obtain a work permit before being able to achieve their goal of moving to the UK, bringing skills and contacts from home, to generate an income and create a balanced life in a new country. This was highlighted during the springboard session and the coach and coachee agreed that the start of the ongoing coaching process would be delayed. The work permit was a legal issue to be handled by legal professionals. In this case the client was happy to resolve these issues without the coach's support.

During this springboard session the coach highlighted some leads for the client to investigate in the meantime. It transpired that one of the leads enabled employment and a temporary work permit for the client who started the ongoing coaching process a month later. However, in most cases the springboard session is straight forward, leading directly to an on-going coaching relationship.

Preliminary foundation

Some coaches insist that the foundation session is conducted face to face. This session is normally a longer session – approximately two hours. If a client and coach are in different locations the coach may suggest that the first telephone coaching session covers the equivalent information gained during a two-hour face-to-face consultation.

Further areas that are discussed and clarified in the springboard session are:

♦ Discovery of five viewpoints of a client's future life – VALUE

♦ Clarity of goals and primary focus for the coaching programme

♦ Responsibility and accountability between the client and coach.

The springboard session involves gaining background information and experiences from the client's past to give insights to where they are in the present and what is available to them now. It also highlights the ways forward, levels of engagement in the development, learning and the experience needed to achieve the client's goals.

THE FIVE VIEWPOINTS OF FUTURE LIFE

In order to clarify and define the objectives of the coaching relationship, *Learning to Coach* has created five key guiding viewpoints to discover the future life that the client wishes to achieve.

The five viewpoints of life are showed by the acronym VALUE – the underlying reason that most clients commission coaching is to find a greater sense of value and enhancement to their life.

The five viewpoints are:

V – values
A – attitude
L – life purpose
U – understanding
E – engagement.

Values

When trying to discover the true values of a client it is important to know to distinguish between inherited values and values that they hold for their future lives. It is also essential for the coach to get beyond general life values – such as honesty, integrity and truth. Although these values are highly regarded in all societies, a coach needs to go beyond the values demanded by culture, society and family principles to discover values that are specific to their client. Much of the terms, names and language that is established in the springboard session will expand during the coaching process between the coach and coachee. It may not mean anything to the outside world but it is meaningful and an instantly recognised shorthand between the client and the coach.

Two questions help to clarify a client's values using negative and positive situations to give clues to deeper, more personal values.

1)   What do you feel are important values in your own life and how do you know when they are being honoured?
2)   What really irritates you about people's behaviour or actions?

Values exercise

Ask your client to sit comfortably and recount events and occasions that bring happy memories to mind and occasions, actions, behaviours or attitudes that have upset them. The coach will need to note their verbal and non-verbal language. Very often the situations that upset people are the reverse of the situations that highlight the client's values.

There are times when a client may be illustrating the same value in both positive and negative ways. For example, Luke feels angry if a person in a group is ignored and their contribution is dismissed. This highlights that he values difference and diversity. Luke also believes that everyone needs to be accepted for who they are and that their contribution should be respected even if he doesn't agree with them.

The reverse situation for Luke was highlighted when he recalled being asked to help organise part of a friend's wedding with another guest he had never met before. When they were introduced they could not agree on the arrangements. However, they finally recognised that they were very good at doing different things and complemented each other's skills. Time was short and they agreed to divide the work according to who was best suited for the task and deferred to each other's superior knowledge when necessary. They started by being very efficient – and 'male' – as Luke expressed it, but soon realised that they were doing a really good job. They had agreed to disagree, but came to respect each other's differences and strengths. Luke said that because he knew that his values were being honoured it felt easy to create something special for a friend's wedding with a total stranger who later became a great friend.

Sets of values

In the above example, Luke acknowledged his values of acceptance, recognition, respect, difference and diversity reoccurring in both negative and positive events. On this occasion Luke decided that it felt good to group these values together to produce his own meaningful value which he named 'welcome'. This was part of a set of values that were specific to him – values that had been growing throughout adulthood and that he wished to take forward into his future life.

Very often, clients need encouragement to recognise their values. To help begin the process of clarifying a coachee's personal values, a sample value list is outlined below:

Achievements	Environment	Recognition
Adventure	Freedom	Risk-taking
Altruism	Fun	Security
Commitment	Humour	Self-expression
Community	Loyalty	Sensuality
Connecting	Openness	Spirituality
Creativity	Privacy	

COACHING HOMEWORK

What are your three top values?

What names are you giving them that are meaningful for you?

Using the Values exercise, experiment with at least one friend to discover their values. Identify their top three values and give them names that are meaningful to use in the future coaching sessions.

Attitude

A client's attitudes influence and overshadow many decisions and experiences they have had in the past, and the way in which they approach the future. Attitude is a state of being – the way a person thinks and feels about things. Clients are often unaware of some of their attitudes and how they affect different relationships and events. A coach needs to be honest enough to point out a client's negative attitudes as well as acknowledging the positive attitudes to increase learning and development.

For example, Harry sought coaching to help him work towards a promotion. He usually worked late, his family were seeing very little of him and being desk bound was affecting his health. Harry also had a quirky sense of humour, which not everyone appreciated. Even though he was acknowledged as good at his job, others were being promoted over him. It was felt that his attitudes, which often came out in his jokes, were detrimental for more senior positions. Harry's coach pointed out the attitudes that could be misconstrued by others and helped him to gain insights into other views. The coach then needed to help Harry to form different attitudes. In his case, it was discovered that Harry used humour as a way of overcoming his shyness.

For Harry, as with many clients, living and working in the 21st century is a question of juggling the demands of work, family, expectations, wants and needs. This commonly requires a re-adjustment to a client's attitudes to life. They may need to change their attitude and be courageous to ask for a pay rise, or to relax and not worry what others may think because the ironing is not done.

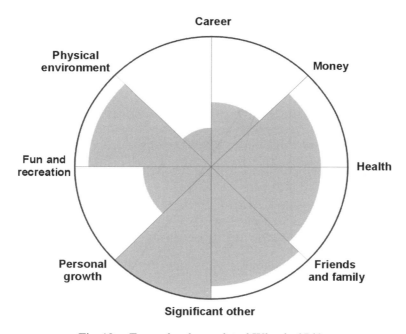

Fig. 18.   Example of completed Wheel of Life.

Creating structure and balance
Structures can help a client to improve the order and balance of their life. Particular areas to tackle are:

♦   Health

♦   Romance/significant other

♦   Physical environment

- Money

- Personal learning and growth

- Fun and recreation

- Career

- Family and friends.

The following questions can help to establish what a client's attitudes are and how to re-calibrate them to get a full, balanced and enjoyable lifestyle.

- What do you find boring that you have to do on a regular basis?

- If money were no object, how would you like your daily life to be?

- What are you tolerating that you would like to change to improve your quality of life?

- In each of these eight areas, name one action that you could take that would improve the quality of your life?

- In each of these eight areas, name one attitude and state of being that you could take to improve your quality of life?

- What practices do you want to make a regular part of your life?

- What changes in attitude and action are you committed to for the improvement of your quality of life?

To help clarify what changes of attitude a client needs the following list of questions encourage additional exploration and insights:

Health

- If you were taking 100 per cent care of yourself, what would you be doing differently in your life that you are not doing currently?

- What would you need to add to your daily routine to ensure that you are as physically and mentally healthy as you can be?

Romance/significant other

- What brings romance into your life?

- What do you need to do to leave 'life' behind and spend quality time with your partner?

Physical environment

- What would make your physical environment perfect for you?

- What have you been planning to do for a long time to improve your physical environment?

Money

- Are all your business and financial matters up to date?

- What is your plan for your future financial security?

Personal learning and growth

- What have you always promised yourself that you will learn 'one day'?

- What don't you do any more that you have enjoyed in the past?

Fun and recreation

- What is a fun day for you and when did you last do it?

- What did you do in the past that you don't do any more?

Career

- What do you long for in your career?

- What does work have to do for you apart from earning you money?

Family and friends

♦ What ensures the most enjoyment when you are with your friends and family?

♦ What allows you to have genuine quality time to enjoy your family and friends?

These are only sample questions. Coaches will discover other avenues and questions they find to be of great value and benefit to their clients during the coaching process.

COACHING HOMEWORK

Complete your own wheel of life. Blank template Fig 27 page 171.

Setting priorities
A coachee then needs to decide what is important in each of these eight areas of their life and what action they need to take (or attitude they need to develop) in order to bring this increased quality to their life. For example, if your client knows that they are leading an un-healthy life through lack of exercise, a desk bound job and irregular eating habits, they may decide that a healthier lifestyle will bring more balance. In order to achieve this balance they need to find a form of exercise that fits easily with their life demands, reassess their eating habits and find opportunities throughout the day to leave their desk at regular intervals.

It is helpful for the coachee to list under each heading what daily habits and regular actions are needed to create a more balanced life. A blank form – 'Daily habits to form a balanced and fulfilled life' – is provided in Chapter 6 to help focus the client's actions and review on a regular basis.

COACHING HOMEWORK

Ask five friends or colleagues what they think your attitude to yourself, life and the world around you is.

What attitudes would you like to change and develop?

Life purpose

It is amazing how many people know where they would like their careers to be in five years time, or how their business will look in the long-term, but rarely have envisaged or planned their personal future. For example, family life, contribution to the community at large, the ways in which to live their dreams or the legacy they would like to leave behind. These do not have to be complicated. It just has to make sense to the client. Here are two questions that can help to provoke these thoughts:

♦ If your family wrote an epitaph to you today, what would they write?

♦ What would you *like* them to write?

Life purpose is about answering the question 'why am I here?' 'What talents and gifts do I have that I can give to others?' Also, 'Who do I need to be for the future?' This does not mean a total re-invention of a client's personality. The springboard session is a wonderful opportunity for the client to take the time to reflect on were they are and what they need to do to be better prepared for the future. When thinking about the future it is very important for the client to know that there is a purpose in their lives.

Recognising life purpose

For example, Kate, when asked the question 'What do your friends, family and work colleagues come to you for?' realised that they came to find a sense of balance, harmony and simplicity. In fact these were strong values for her. She was known for cutting through the dross of life and adding fun to any given situation.

Exercise to clarify purpose

To clarify her purpose in life, Kate was asked to imagine that she felt a great urge to say something to a group of strangers, and started talking to them. The coach asked the questions:

♦   What was so important that you felt you had to share it with others?

♦   What impact did your message have on the group?

Kate wanted to tell the strangers that there is always a choice as to how complicated and difficult we want our life to be. She also stated that we have to acknowledge the positive and negative impact that we have on those around us. Kate felt extremely grateful that she had been helped in the past to embrace all the realities of life, both joyful and difficult. She felt that the reason many people came to her was because they felt more relaxed with her – 'You seem to manage to cut away all the dross and find the kernel'. She described her life purpose as being like an Italian church full of old frescoes, bright glass, newly lit candles, cool air and a hushed atmosphere where people could come and sit, gather their thoughts and find peace and simplicity.

Kate felt her life purpose was to bring harmony and a sense of release in tough times to those around her. She felt strongly that, creating and generating simplicity in life, and cutting out the hype and drama of situations was what she did naturally. She felt that this was the most positive thing that she could do for herself, for her family and those she came in contact with on a daily basis. Her legacy was to leave behind memories and experiences for others that demonstrated you could live a full, exciting life and yet keep it simple.

Kate gave a name for her future improved self – 'Dust buster' – which she said was a combination of who she was in the present with the extra benefits of learning and development that she wanted for herself. These two realisations, combined with the commitments that Kate had made to herself, added an extra feeling of purpose and sense to her world.

COACHING HOMEWORK

What would you like your friends and family to say about you in an epitaph?

What is your purpose in life?

Understanding

The springboard session offers a rare time for coachees to be able to reflect upon and begin to understand how and why they act in certain ways. It gives them the opportunity to make choices between positive and negative actions and thoughts. It also begins a process of defining what a coachee can learn and develop to help them achieve their future life goals. For example, in Harry's case he wanted to be promoted. He took the opportunity to understand his actions and reactions that were helpful or detrimental to his situation.

Harry's quirky sense of humour covered his natural shyness with work colleagues. His shyness, he began to understand in the springboard session, came from being a self-contained child whose family moved a lot during his childhood due to his father's profession. Harry was good at project work and loved being left to his own devices, and later presenting the job to the team when it was finished. He felt vulnerable and anxious meeting new people and found it difficult to interact on a long-term basis. Harry's shyness and resulting behaviours were creating a barrier that prevented him from gaining his goal and benefiting from the coaching process if not addressed.

Barriers to the coaching process

Barriers to the coaching process created by the client, are usually signs of an inner self-sabotaging voice, deconstructive behaviour or some form of what is popularly termed 'gremlins'. It is very important that the coach helps to identify gremlin behaviour and allows the client to discover and accept the negative power and dynamics that these behaviours precipitate in their life.

During the springboard session the coach will hear clues as to possible self-sabotaging reasoning and understanding by the client. This can be shown through both verbal and non-verbal listening skills when asking about past successes and failures experienced. Being able to identify these gremlins and name them for future reference in the coaching relationship enables the client to recognise the difference between themselves as a gremlin-driven client and themselves as a gremlin-free purposeful client.

The voices of resistance

In order to understand the ways in which resistance may be presented during a coaching session, there follows a list of examples given by clients that alert the coach that they may be facing resistance rather than an honest enquiry from the client:

♦ The coachee floods the coaching session with unnecessary detail and story.

♦ The coachee asks for more detail or explanation from the coach.

- The coachee says they do not have time.

- The coachee reminds the coach that they live in the real world and need practical, quick suggestions.

- The coachee becomes angry or begins to defend their stance with aggression.

- The coachee keeps on saying that they are confused, and they want clarity.

- The coachee uses silence as a way of not communicating rather than a way of reflecting.

- The coachee intellectualises situations rather than examining intangible feelings.

- The coachee hides behind a moralising attitude and recounts other people's stories and agendas, not their own.

The forms of resistance listed above may be disguising some underlying concerns that the coachee has. For example:

- Issues of control, usually losing it.

- A sense of vulnerability and anxiety.

- Fear of being perceived as weak.

- Wanting confirmation rather than change.

- Disloyalty to values.

- A fear of the unknown.

- A sense of shame for past behaviours.

- Uncomfortable with the possible conflict of new habits and behaviours.

◆   Being fully accountable and responsible for themselves as an adult.

◆   Feelings of guilt.

Organisations, communities and families all have 'gremlin' comments that coaches need to listen for and acknowledge in order that for the client to gain a full insight into the ways that unconscious and habitual negative behaviour can be colluded with.

Gremlins

It is important to realise that the main aim of a gremlin is to keep the status quo. Often, at times of sabotaging patterns, the coach needs to highlight the ways in which a client's values, broader agenda and future vision of life are being compromised. Naming a gremlin also creates a metaphor that is instantly recognisable and meaningful to the coach and the client.

Sometimes there is one overriding attitude or pattern for the client – perhaps they often say 'there is never enough', 'I'm never enough', 'I can't give enough' or 'I always drive myself hard. If I don't drive myself hard I'm a failure', 'If people don't drive themselves hard enough they're not contributing'. Some examples of gremlins like to these are discussed by Richard D Carson in his book *Taming Your Gremlin* or *The little Saboteur* by Marco Von Munchhausen. Carson chooses the names to describe certain gremlins – such as 'The General', 'The Hulk' and 'The Grim Reaper'.

Other clients understand their gremlin a different way. For example, Kate came to the conclusion that her general attitudes were demonstrated in a variety of ways. On further investigation she decided that she was as likely to hear a 'little two-year-old' sabotaging voice as she was an 'adult doubting Thomas' voice. Her decision was to christen her gremlin behaviour and voice 'The Addams Family' – a behaviour that was charming (but out of touch with reality), archaic, judgemental, limiting in behaviour, stuck in a time-warp and proud of it. Kate acknowledged the Addams Family for what they were, and the affect they could have on her actions and decision-making. By naming them she was able to counteract their effect and follow her goals for a future life with courage, conviction and energy.

Using humour

When naming a gremlin it is important that the chosen label means something to the client in order to illustrate limiting behaviour or to become a shorthand between the coach and the client. Using humour to name the gremlin creates a lightness and instant point of reference for the client if the gremlin behaviour needs to be exposed by the coach or coachee. For example, Harry's gremlin became known as 'Smegel with sunglasses'. The character Smegel from *The Lord of the Rings* represented the isolated, multi personalities that Harry had when feeling threatened. Harry decided if Smegel wore sunglasses he would be happier to come out and enjoy the sunshine, experience life and have fun.

COACHING HOMEWORK

What are your self-sabotaging patterns? Complete the following:

My gremlin's name is:

My gremlin often says:

Engagement

When clients are sharing and deciding their goals and future, the coach needs to know what level of commitment they are willing to expend. A good question to extrapolate this is:

'What is so engaging and compelling about this vision and these goals that you are willing to do all that is necessary in both the good and bad times?'

The clients themselves need to know that they are willing to do all that is necessary to learn, experience and develop. Some clients come with definite goals and others are not so clear, but they need to know what form the results of their decisions and commitments might take.

Recognising barriers to learning
The springboard session is a good opportunity for the coach and coachee to discover situations or beliefs that might jeopardise new experiences and learning. For example, one of Kate's goals for coaching was to move to Italy to find work there. She committed to sign up for Italian lessons, tell her work colleagues that she would like to practise her conversation with them and would ask the manager if they would consider to transfer her to one of the offices in Italy for a six-month trial period. Kate was asked how engaged she was in achieving this goal considering she had a tough work load at the moment and decided she was useless at learning languages.

'What is so compelling about this goal of living and working in Italy other than your vision of sitting on the pavement after work watching the Italians promenade?'

Being realistic
After further consideration Kate came to the conclusion that she had really only taken a History of Art degree for the Italian art and history. She'd had a dream since childhood to live in Italy and this was as good as any time to go and do it. Kate needed to know that her decision to go to Italy did not mean she was planning never to return to the UK. It was a trial not a life sentence, and she did not have to be a perfect Italian speaker or sell up her home to be successful and achieve it. In this way, Kate had mapped out her level of engagement.

The following three questions, can help a client to map out their levels of engagement in their goals and visions.

♦   Where can you 'not go' to lessen your engagement in achieving this?

♦   What do you need to say 'Yes' to in order to open yourself up to new opportunities?

♦   What do you need to say 'No' to in order to open yourself up to new opportunities?

GOALS AND PRIMARY FOCUS FOR COACHING

To make coaching beneficial, there needs to be a clear focus for the process. It may be that a client comes with the desire to have a sense of clarity for the next phase of their life. Their goal is simply 'to have clarity'. It may be a definite goal such as changing jobs, setting up a business, increasing income generations, achieving more balance or creating a new sense of ease for their future commitments and life.

Whatever a client chooses as their goals and primary focus to life, it is a good idea to ask a client to reveal their goals at the beginning of the springboard session (if it has not already been discussed at the initial contact stage). A client's goals can then be reviewed at the end of the springboard session to establish that these are the goals that the client really wants for themselves, the commitment they have to them and the implications of achieving them.

The three basic questions needed to establish goals and achieving them are:

(1) What would make them SMART goals?
(2) What do you currently have to achieve them?
(3) What do you need to have to achieve them?

(1) To establish goals, the coachee needs to consider if they are SMART goals:

S – specific
M – measurable
A – achievable
R – realistic
T – time-tied

(2) and (3) In order to decide what actions are needed to achieve a goal, the coach needs to discover what the coachee already has available to them, what they will need in addition and what support structures they need to help them in their quest. This includes designing structures that include requests to the coach in the way they interact with the client.

The three areas to review are:

♦ People

♦ Places

♦ Other factors.

Coaching through these points will enable an action plan to emerge. The Coaches toolkit in Chapter 6 includes a blank form – 'Goals – resources, planning, support structure' – to aid the stages in this process. The form allows for the different stages of the action plan to be recorded and linked to the time-tied element of the SMART goal checklist for future learning.

RESPONSIBILITY OF COACH AND COACHEE

The coach

It is the responsibility of the coach to act professionally with their client and to make sure that they work with them in any way that supports them in achieving their objectives. The coach needs to be clear and honest with their clients when the relationship is not working, if professional boundaries are infringed and when the client is side stepping their agenda or values in any way.

The coach needs to be aware of the impact that coaching will have on a) their client and b) on other people in the client's life. Although the coaching is carried out on a one-to-one basis, the coachee's agenda will invariably have effects on others that may need to be considered and addressed in the most appropriate ways.

The coach needs to know what will make the coaching process valuable for the coachee, what might hinder the process and other information that will aid and suit an individual client. In short, the coach needs to know how to achieve a valuable, compelling and dynamic relationship with their client.

The coachee

The coachee is responsible for their learning and development during the coaching process. At all times they need to be honest with the coach. They should tell the coach when they are worried or upset by anything in the coaching sessions – or when the coaching relationship is not working fully for them. The coaching relationship is a professional relationship and therefore should be respected by both coach and coachee.

There are occasions when actions affect more than one person, and others may need to be included in the coaching process. The coachee needs to be aware of the impact of their decisions and development on other people in their life and to be honest and open with the coach about any concerns or additional support they may need as a result. For example, there are times when the coach offers a client the opportunity to come together with their partner to be coached on actions and decisions that are connected to both parties – for instance in the case of changing lifestyle, job, retiring or relocating.

This does not mean that the one-to-one coaching relationship is ended and will be replaced by a couple coaching relationship. It simply enables the couple to have a clear, safe, neutral space to be able to review and discuss the issues at hand. These discussions may only last for one or two sessions, or they may go on for longer periods, depending on the client's wishes. Again, the coachee is responsible for letting the coach know what will make this relationship the most valuable, compelling and dynamic for them.

Springboard session information

A blank form is included in the Coaches toolkit (Chapter 6) to record the information gathered at the springboard session. Using a combination of examples given in this chapter a completed form would look something like this:

Springboard session	
V – Values	'Welcome' – Luke
A – Attitude	Be sensitive to others and be courageous to connect with others – Harry
L – Life purpose	Keep it simple and improve Kate 'Dust buster' – Kate

U – Understanding   Gremlin: Smegel with sunglasses and come out and live life in the open – Harry

E – Engagement   Experiencing the dream as a trial not a life sentence – Katie

Goals and Primary Focus

1) Moving and working in Italy – Kate
2) New promotion and healthy, balanced life – Harry

Coaching Relationship – How do you want the coach to be?
Tell me as you see it is and challenging – Harry
Barriers/structures/help
Ask me each week what I have learnt in Italian – Kate
Logistics – Telephone coaching 3 x 40 mins calls on 1st/2nd/3rd week of month.
Review after 3 months – Luke

IN SUMMARY

The springboard session:

♦ is a chance to gather background information, to reflect on the present and to prepare for what is needed in the future

♦ is an opportunity to review the coachee's VALUE

♦ should highlight gremlins and other barriers to coaching, learning and developing

♦ needs to establish goals and focus for coaching sessions and any form of measurements

♦ will discover the best ways for a coach to support their coachee.

4
The Coaching Process

The coaching process is the third step in building the coaching relationship (Fig. 1). Throughout the coaching process, the coach will aim to uphold the client's bigger purpose and goals by referring to the values, attitude, life purpose, understanding and engagement (V-A-L-U-E) highlighted by the client. The information and insights gathered during the springboard session form the foundation to begin the ongoing coaching process.

CREATING BALANCE

It is part of the skill and responsibility of the coach to be able to balance the day-to-day 'stuff' that the client brings to each session, with the goals, primary focus and broader vision that the coachee wants for their life. It is very easy for the coachee to get bogged down with 'life' (such as day-to-day agendas and goals) in a way that drowns out the big 'A' agenda they have come to coaching to achieve. If the coach is not assiduous during the coaching sessions they may find themselves colluding in these problems of niggles, emergencies and unforeseen circumstances at the expense of the broader purpose. The coach needs to be able to raise the client's head out of the morass of the moment and take the broader perspective to gain in-depth learning from the situation, rather than just sorting it out with a 'sticking plaster' in the short-term.

If a coach focuses on the immediate concerns of their client they will only be helping the client to fire fight situations. A more valuable exercise is to look at the causes and effects and ask questions such as 'what is underneath or beyond the presenting situation of the day' in order to learn and develop from the experiences and to move forward with a greater impact and lasting achievement.

Little agenda   **Big agenda**

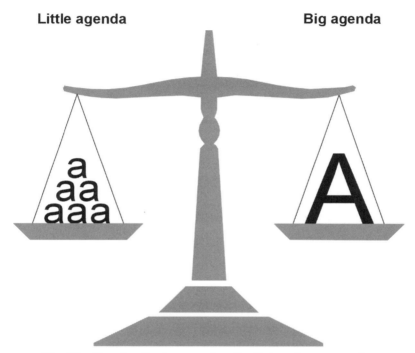

Fig. 19.   Keeping the focus on the client's broader purpose by balancing big and little agendas.

A coach needs to have a sense of balance in order to make the coaching process of maximum benefit to their client. The balance of a client's big 'A' (goals and purpose) and the little 'a' (day-to-day) agenda of life.

Maintaining focus

In order to hold the clients big 'A' agenda the coach must not get swamped and distracted by the client's day-to-day little 'a' agenda. They will need to be able to take their client and themselves above the 'stuff' of the coaching session and look at the broader picture to gain perspective. The meta/helicopter view creates a different perspective – it frees up the client's limited thinking and experience of situations and draws the focus away from the issue in hand to see it in relation to the whole. For example, if a client is suddenly insistent that they must take a bigger mortgage to provide the family with a more spacious home, the coach may ask the client how that fits in to their desired goals of decreasing family debt and working less hours. The coach takes the coachee to look from an overall perspective to understand the consequences of a proposed action. They are gaining a meta view.

This chapter reviews the different factors that constitute the ongoing coaching process. They are:

♦   Models for coaching

♦   Facilitating planning

♦   Providing a sustainable relationship

♦   Closure.

MODELS FOR COACHING

There are many different models and strategies that have been developed to create a framework to follow through a coaching session. They range from step-by-step coaching models, such as the GROW model or 3-step coaching process, to a model that gives a variety of coaching skills and tools that can be used flexibly together – as in the co-Active coaching model by the Coaches Training Institute (CTI). The GROW model is based on the following:

G – goal – setting for the short- and long-term
R – reality – checking to explore the current situation
O – options – alternative strategies or courses of action
W – will – what strategy or action is to be done when, by whom and the will to do it

The 3-step model is based on a more flexible template of:

1. Who?
Get to know the client or individual, and their values, skills, experience, aspirations, and fears. For a company these might also include purpose, product revenue and profit margins.

2. What?
Clarify the goals. Where did the goals come from? Are they really the client's and do they fit with their core values? No 'should' or 'must' here about the aims and objectives of goal setting – they must truly be wants and ambitions to seek this change.

3. How?
Strategies to get there. What needs to be done to close the gap between the current position and where the client wants to be? The client needs to recognise this from within. Break goals down into manageable projects and prioritise them. Identifying with the issues also helps to close the gaps.

The CTI Co-active coaching model has flexible and interlinked skills and tools for the client and coach to use together based on an holistic view of issues of balance, fulfilment and process in all aspects of personal and professional life.

All professional coaches will train within the models in order to learn their skills and develop. In time, most coaches will become used to working with an array of tools and skills that they can perfect during their commitment to continuous professional development and supervision. One analogy showing this professional development would be to look at the work of two famous artists in the 20th century who both broadened the horizons of art in general. They were Pablo Picasso and Piet Mondrian. Both had a solid classical art training and were excellent draftsmen in their own right and could not have achieved their experience and progress in modern art without this knowledge. Their figurative art, especially the portraits by Picasso between 1914–1918 and Mondrian's early landscapes, demonstrates this fact. However, they both chose to explore the additional ways that visual art could be exercised to coincide with the changing world they found themselves in. Professional external coaches tend to follow the same path – exploring, being curious and never forgetting that life is about learning. There are some organisations that create their own coaching models to use the language and culture of their individual organisation. In cases like these, internal coaches are usually bound to using these models. However, any progressive organisation will encourage new tools, skills and ideas being incorporated as they see fit.

Some organisations have a preference of coaching models but the basic broad strategies for coaching are the same. They are:

♦ Recognising and using the client's gifts and talents

♦ Moving to an action based environment

♦ Deciding what has to be added and what has to be taken away to progress

♦ Defining where the client can get support (emotional, financial, physical etc).

Questions that support the basic broad strategy
This basic broad strategy is supported by client's questions such as:

♦ 'What am I putting up with?' – By identifying the little problems that interfere with life, and removing them, gives us clarity to move on to more major blocks.

- ◆ 'Who am I to other people?' – Trying to identify where the client's standing among their contemporaries or how they are perceived (or perceive themselves).

- ◆ 'What is the essence of my dream/goals/purpose in life?' – What is the client doing with their life and how can they start to live in ways that are meaningful for them.

- ◆ 'Why am I not doing this already?' – What is the reality of their true levels of engagement? It can be a case of the coaching process enabling them to review their values (VALUE), or in the case of organisations, their mission, values and strategy.

The questions listed here are for illustration only. It is best for the coach to chose their own questions based on the meaningful language and understanding that they created in the springboard session. If, going through these steps, the coachee is unsure or undecided, then the coach needs to take them back to the previous stage to re-gain deeper insights and understanding that will spring the coachee forward again.

The work presented in this book is based on a review of many coaching books and models, the continual development of coaching as a profession and the experience of coaches in the field. In an endeavour to bring some cohesion and understanding to the practice of coaching and its effectiveness and value, it has been revealed that the only word or term common to all (with the same meaning within the word) was 'question'. However, by comparing and over laying the models, language and terms often used solely to create a registered product that could be a business income stream, some similarities did come to light.

The coaching model illustrated in Figure 7, page 23, creates a framework that both experienced and novice coaches can work with, maintaining a structure as well as giving flexibility to coaching sessions for both individuals and an organisational third party or for sponsored coaching. As with the illustration, the coaching structure is based on a jigsaw, with everything interlinking and only effective when all parts have been completed. The process can be carried out in a linear fashion, but the use of the jigsaw motif is a reminder that the parts can be revisited and recalibrated at any stage. The experience of action and the learning from that experience both encourage reflection and subtle changes.

Having completed the springboard phase in the last chapter, and before embarking on facilitating the planning of the coaching process, it would now be a good time to look at the process of learning that everyone experiences.

PROCESS OF LEARNING

There are four steps in the learning process:

1. Unconscious incompetence
2. Conscious incompetence
3. Conscious competence
4. Unconscious competence.

Fig. 20. Process of learning.

The behaviours and attitudes that illustrate these four different stages are:

1. Unconscious incompetence
   Personal   Don't know/don't care
   At work   Enthusiastic beginner

2. Conscious incompetence
   Personal   i.e. Learning to drive and you realise you are unable
   At work   Disillusioned learner

3. Conscious competence
   Personal   Can drive car but still needs to think about it
   At work   Reluctant contributor

4. Unconscious competence
   Personal   Driving automatically
   At work   Peak performers

Fig. 21.   Facilitate planning – 2nd key phase of coaching process.

FACILITATE PLANNING

Facilitate planning is the 2nd key phase of the coaching process. The motivation and engagement of the coachee during the coaching process needs be 'aligned' or 'congruent' for them in order to facilitate planning of actions. For each person to learn and gain from the experience, they need to address the efforts and changes that are required on all levels. There are five logical levels, which are:

PURPOSE – (who/what else?)

IDENTITY – (who?)

VALUES/BELIEFS – (why?)

CAPABILITIES/SKILLS/COMPETENCIES – (how?)

BEHAVIOUR – (what?)

ENVIRONMENT – (where/when?)

One step at a time

When reviewing the goals and issues that a coachee raises, the prior level needs to be addressed first. For example, Mary wanted to decide the next stage of her life, moving from 'City career Mum' to 'Family Mum with a purpose' (Purpose). In order to decide her purpose, she needed to look at who she was (Identity), which in turned asked what her values and beliefs were now, and then which of her capabilities, skills and competencies she wanted to use in the next stage of her life and so on. To be fully engaged, clients need to be aligned and congruent on all of these levels.

Creating a Framework

In order to achieve this a framework is needed to provide a coaching decision-making process to give clients a well-formed outcome. Such a framework is outlined in *Move on Up* by Liz Reed – the first mentor coach to establish a coaching course for adult learning that was accredited by a UK university.

Decision-making for a well-formed outcome is a series of questions testing the well-formedness of plans for changing from a *present state* to a *desired state*.

These are outlined below. You should ask the first three questions in the order given, the other six questions may be asked in any order appropriate.

1. What do you want?
(must be stated in the *positive*)

2. How will you know when you have achieved it?
(i.e. describe the feelings you will experience then.)

3. How will others know that you have it?
(i.e. how will you demonstrate it publicly?)

4. Can you initiate it and maintain it yourself?
(what, or who, could stop you?)

5. Is it appropriate for every context?
(do you want it all the time? – everywhere? – with everybody or not?)

6. Will you be able to keep the secondary gains you enjoy at present?
(what will you have to give up?)

7. Will it be worth the effort/time/money you will have to devote to attaining it?
(what will it cost you?)

8. How will getting this affect your present relationships?

9. How will the change affect your self-image?

A well-informed outcome is both attainable and worth attaining.

PREPARATIONS FOR COACHING

Before each coaching session, whether the coaching takes place face to face or over the telephone, it is helpful for the coach to be up to speed with the intervening events that the coachee has experienced since the last session.

A preparation form asks the coachee questions such as:

♦   What have I accomplished since our last session?

♦   What didn't I get done, but intended to?

♦   What are the challenges and problems I am facing now?

♦   What are the opportunities available to me right now?

♦   What great insights have I had during the period?

♦   What do I feel grateful for right now?

♦   What do I specifically want to be coached on during the session?

The form is not meant to be a task and hard chore. It is an opportunity for the client to be able to keep track of where they are emotionally, how they are being able to focus on their aims and objectives, and to register any other points of reference that are helping or hindering progress.

Realistic timeframe
It is best to give the client time to complete the preparation (prep) form and the coach the opportunity to assess the information, especially if there are any requests from the client. The usual request is that the

prep form is completed and returned to the coach 24 hours before the next coaching session.

This notice period gives the coachee the chance to:

♦ Complete the form without 'last minute' time pressures before the session

♦ Consider their progress and the implications

♦ Decide if they need to take actions, or tie up loose ends

♦ Know what they want to focus on in the next coaching session.

Receiving the prep form 24 hours before the next coaching session gives the coach a chance to:

♦ Read the form without 'last minute' pressures and be up to speed with their client

♦ Note any insights that they might have to share with the client

♦ Know what is the important focus for the client in the coming session

♦ Be prepared to be flexible during the coaching session, beyond the planned agenda cited on the prep form – 24 hours has elapsed and 'things' can move forward in that time period.

An important point to remember is that a coach can gain much information about their client's current situation from the prep form – even if it is not completed. It could be the client forgot or that they hate filling out forms. Are they too busy due to the pressure of life? Do they try to complete the form perfectly? There is no judgement to be made over a missed prep form – but it can give an insight into old and new behaviours and attitudes.

Coach   **Client**

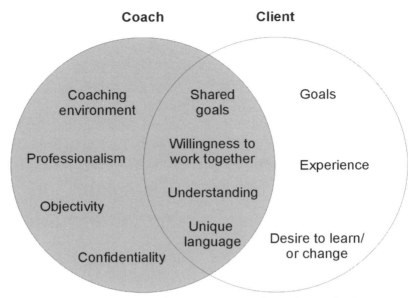

Fig. 22.   The coaching process grows from the coachee's
own qualities and style.

Coaches need to remember to coach their clients from where they are
and not from where the coach would like them to be.

REMAINING IMPARTIAL

On one side, (see Figure 22) the coach offers a coaching environment,
professionalism, objectivity and confidentiality and on the other side,
the coachee chooses to experience, learn and change to achieve their
goals. The coaching process is controlled by the coachee, who consents
to sharing goals, understanding and a willingness to work together, and
this creates a unique language between the coach and coachee. Mean-
while the coach remains static – inviting the coachee in to the coaching
space that they hold.

In the case of the prep form, actions speak louder than words. This
process often illustrates other behaviours beyond bringing the coach

up to speed on circumstances. It is a good barometer of the state of mind that the client is presently in. For example:

♦ Is your client normally timely in sending you the prep form?

♦ What has happened to make it arrive only half an hour before your coaching session on this particular occasion?

♦ Does your client always send the prep form late giving the coach no chance to read before a session?

♦ Does your client have a habit of emailing you the form just before the coaching session even after you have explained that you are unable to download emails during your coaching days?

♦ Does your client find any of the questions embarrassing or frightening to think about and answer? For example insights, gratitude, what they are intending to do.

As with all interactions within the coaching relationship, whatever happens to the prep form is indicative of the client's present circumstance and state of being. The prep form is a great opportunity for the coach to increase their awareness and better support their client in the coaching process.

COACHING HOMEWORK

Look at the prep form in the coach's tool kit (see Chapter 6) and:

a) Use it with your clients
Question:
What benefit did your clients gain from completing the prep form?
What insights and benefits did you as a coach gain from the prep form?

b) Improve and design your own prep form for future use with your coachees.

PROVIDE A SUSTAINABLE RELATIONSHIP

Fig. 23.   Provide a sustainable relationship – 3rd key phase
of coaching process.

Providing a sustainable relationship is the 3rd phase of the coaching process. The secret to sustaining a dynamic relationship is for the coach to know how to be flexible in response to the client's changing awareness, learning and experience of the coaching process.

The peaks and plateaus of a coaching session

As in all processes of learning and change, there are times of peaks and plateaus. For some clients, clarifying, setting goals and planning the action is exciting. It gives them a purpose and something to aim for and work towards. Maybe the goal is life changing, the realisation of a dream or sorting the wheat from the chaff of their life. Whatever the reason, the client is fired up and ready to go. Now they have to live through the process of taking action, experiencing the course of their decision-making and learning from the consequences.

To gain the maximum benefit from the coaching process, the client will need to pass through four distinct and conscious periods in their experiences.

1) Identify and clarify
2) Take action
3) Experience the consequences
4) Recalibrate and renew behaviour

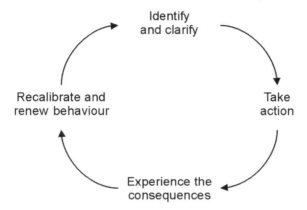

Fig. 24.   The cycle of learning and experience during
the coaching process.

A continuous journey

Sometimes this learning is like travelling at high speed. It is fast and the journey happens so quickly that a client wonders how they got there, although they are thrilled to have arrived. At other times the journey is a slow and ponderous process. Actions throw up more questions and life throws up barriers from seemingly nowhere. Motivation dips and the client wonders 'why bother'? Suddenly they find their commitment is waning.

Whatever stage of the coaching process the client is in, they need to learn from their experiences. During the peak times the coach and client may need to consciously go back and analyse what is happening to imbed the learning for the future and to keep the momentum strong for the tougher times. In the plateaus, it can seem as though there is nothing to do but wait for outside influences to resolve themselves. All these experiences, both positive and negative, need to be examined for what they really mean to the client. Often the most difficult part of the process is sustaining the action.

LEARNING FROM ACTION AND EXPERIENCE

Learning or changing new behaviours and attitudes can create tension and frustration for clients. The coach needs to encourage their client to accept that learning comes from experience – and not necessarily from getting the desired results straight away. For example, Luke, who held the personal value of 'welcome' (see page 87) felt that everyone needed to be accepted for who and what they were. During the coaching process, this value was highlighted as leaving Luke open to accepting situations or other people's attitudes that were detrimental. Luke had come to coaching with the primary goal of taking a sabbatical to travel through Africa and to re-visit some of the humanitarian projects he had help to set up ten years earlier. He had taken his organisation through a total restructuring process and wanted a break. The coaching process helped Luke to negotiate time off from work, and put in place a framework to support his department and the organisation at large while he was away.

Luke became aware, while he was reviewing his lines of responsibility, accountability, support and leadership, that he had been too accepting of one of his heads of department. When Luke had been actively living by his values he was understanding of some difficult personal circumstances and business pressures involved, but he did not realise the negative effect it was having on parts of his team. He discovered that the natural lines of responsibility and succession that he had assumed would come into play while he was away, had been disrupted, and he needed to look at his part to rectify the issue.

THE THREE 'A'S OF RE-LEARNING

The three 'A's' of re-learning are awareness, acceptance, and only then, action. When Luke moved into action he was no longer willing to accept less than 100 per cent from all his team. His personal goal to take a sabbatical for three months was in danger of being postponed or cancelled altogether. His efforts to re-adjust his levels of acceptance were felt as a total personality transplant by his colleagues. It was not Luke's intention, but he was viewed as changing from a sympathetic and supportive leader into an insensitive, unaccommodating human dynamo. Illustrating Luke's actions in relation to his value showed that he had been too accepting. Luke's efforts to change meant that he was seen as intolerant and causing a level of friction he was not accustomed too. Luke's coach needed to help him to develop a form of target learning and behaviour that would truly serve to enrich his future.

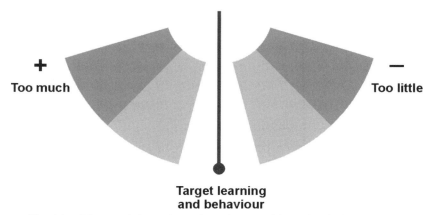

+
Too much

—
Too little

Target learning
and behaviour

Fig. 25.   The pendulum of new learning to achieve the desired results.

RECOGNISING PERSONALITY TYPES

The personal styles and traits of clients will have a bearing on how they manage to deal with the peaks and plateaus of success, failure and the process of learning from them. For example, Kate started the coaching process full of enthusiasm having divided her goal into definable pieces of achievement. The main areas were, managing her money, learning to speak basic Italian and arranging to 'store' her life while she was away. She had given herself a three-month timeline. Kate identified herself as a 'be perfect' person who hated misunderstandings and liked to learn as a 'reflector' – she felt more comfortable learning by listening, reading or observing and preferred to avoid learning situations where she put herself in the limelight.

The first month of coaching was dominated by a heavy workload, the second month by a long planned two-week holiday and the third month started with unforeseen changes giving her a new position at work. Kate began to realise that her financial position was more precarious than she thought. She was still paying back her student loans from her undergraduate and MA degrees, which overshadowed her sense of being a free individual with no ties. The coach kept Kate's goal in focus, but as the coaching proceeded, Kate repeatedly 'forgot' to learn Italian and often came to the sessions full of work highs and lows, too busy to complete any of the responsibilities she had set for herself.

Coach – '*I noticed that you have not been able to complete a prep form before our coaching today – so what do you want to be coached on in this session?*'

Kate – '*Oh I'm so sorry . . . I've been so busy again this week. Time just flies. I guess I have to be straight with you that I haven't done any of the things I said I would . . . Again!*'

Coach – '*Actually Kate – I'm curious as to why that is. No judgement, it's your agenda, but, what is really going on here?*'

RECOGNISING GREMLIN BEHAVIOUR

Kate told the coach she was feeling overwhelmed at the thought of learning Italian. She would never be able to have the level of conversations in Italian that she did in English and that she would be very lonely being in a wonderful ancient Italian city without any friends to chat to or a decent job. On top of that, she felt financial commitments meant that she couldn't really afford to go to Italy and to enjoy herself freely and now she also had a new position at work.

Coach – '*You know Kate, I really hear that you're concerned and edgy about this, but I think I just heard your gremlin step into the coaching session. It doesn't sound like you speaking, but "wee Katie"* (name given to her self-sabotaging, resistance gremlin voice in the springboard session). *What does wee Katie want to say?*'

By highlighting this resistance and using the gremlin's name, the coach enabled Kate to see her thoughts and feelings with more clarity. Following on from the previous review of gremlins in Chapter 3 p. 98, Kate further investigated how her gremlin was trying to keep the status quo.

Kate – '*Wee Katie is saying "Stay at home, you don't have time to sort your money situation out – it's not perfect – it's going to be so embarrassing trying to practise speaking Italian with all my colleagues knowing what I'm doing . . . you work for an Italian company anyway – isn't that enough Italian for you anyway"*.'

Coach – '*What else?*'

Kate – '*Oh . . . packing up and sorting all my stuff out before I go. I know I'm paying for storage space for different bits of furniture, pots and pans I've bought to use in various rented flats . . . I even still have all my notes from University . . . You know talking to you over the phone I feel overwhelmed and flat – I don't know if I really want to go.*'

Coach – '*Wow, it sounds big and I'm not surprised you feel overwhelmed right now. What else adds to this overwhelming feeling?*'

FINDING THE REALITY

By giving Kate the space to clear and voice all her concerns the coach has given her the opportunity to see what is real for her, whether it sounds logical or not.

Coach – *'How are you – right now – in this session Kate?'*
Kate – *'Flat – tied down and flat.'*
Coach – *'I know you're on a hands-free phone, can I ask you to get up and move around the room. You're an active person, who's been tied behind a desk all day.'*
Kate – *'You're right . . . And I haven't seen daylight all day and it is the middle of summer. There's a window here . . . Hey it's sunny and everyone's scuttling along like ants below . . . and a low flying pigeon has just gone past!'*
Coach – *'So, if you were to take a birds eye view of your of all your concerns right now, what perspective would you have?'*

Later . . .

Coach – *'What other perspectives can you think of? Can I suggest one? Since your life purpose is to keep things simple and be "Dust buster" what does that lead you to?'*

The coach has asked permission to intentionally change the physical geography of the session and used incidental information with meaningful language to help Kate, move away from her 'be perfect' attitude and create a more reflective manner, out of the limelight.

Checklist for self-sabotaging patterns
The following questions will help your clients to discover why they may be repeatedly missing actions that they insist they want to achieve:

♦   What can you do to stop procrastinating?

- Who do you need to 'be' instead to override your procrastinating mindset?

- Do you really want this or is it a 'should', 'ought' or 'must'?

- What is really going on for you underneath to sabotage your intended behaviour?

- How are you honouring your V-A-L-U-E by doing – or choosing not to do – these actions?

- Is this a case of over planning and loading of your busy life? OOPS – Over Operational Planning Syndrome.

Resistance to Learning

However willing and trusting the coachee is, there are always moments in the coaching process that throw up unexpected barriers and resistance to learning. These barriers can be shown in many different ways, but coaches need to be aware when they appear in the coaching session and articulate what they see happening to the coachee. This has been explained more fully in Chapter 2. Barriers appear as fear of change, failure or even of the success 'limelight'. Examples of previous experience are voiced or 'Can't teach an old dogs new tricks' syndrome appears, highlighting an unexpected lack of confidence. One of the purposes of working through a springboard session is that the coach and coachee will be able to establish meaningful language, terms and structures that can be used during the coaching process to learn from these barriers and self-sabotaging behaviour to move forward again.

MAINTAINING FLEXIBILITY

There is a danger of inexperienced coaches using a step by step coaching model and feeling they must work through it directly and precisely. They can unconsciously treat the creativity and insights made possible through coaching as a linear process. This is rarely the case – coaching sessions are flexible in thought, word, experience and action. The emphasis in the session often changes when new insights, learning and experience take place. For example, Harry was an enthusiastic coachee who had requested that he spend the session planning the next steps of the coaching. Harry had identified himself as being a 'Be Strong', character that he learnt best in an 'Activist' style and was a 'C' – compliance in DISC. Harry walked into the coaching session a few minutes late, beaming from ear to ear, carrying a small box of chocolates.

Harry – *'Hi, sorry I'm late but I'm so excited . . . I heard this morning that I've been given the promotion . . . The deal we have been working on has been successful . . . I've lost 2lbs since last week . . . and got to the gym . . . all in the garden is smelling rosy . . . so I nipped out to get some- thing to celebrate in this session. Champagne truffles – my favourites to say thank you.'*

Coach – *'I'm so pleased for you. You've put a lot of effort in lately to achieve your goals in such a short time span, and now they seem to have surpassed your expectations. Tell me more, before we start on the forward planning you wanted to work on in this session.'*

Later . . .

Harry – *'So you see I think I've tied everything up now and established some really good new behaviours and habits – so I'm not sure what to be coached next . . . if there's anything for us to do together. Have another chocolate.'*

Coach – *'Thank you . . . and thinking about chocolate, I'm curious to know how you will be re-organising your healthy habits to fit into the new travelling pattern, and how you'll keep your family project in focus?'*

Harry – *'Hum . . . You've got me there . . . I just had a flash of me trying to 'be strong' again and I do need support – some structures*

*– around the changes that are going to take place. Thanks for this . . .
let's see . . .'*

UTILISING LIFE SKILLS

Clients bring to the coaching session, all past experiences, learning, personal styles and behaviours. Their values, attitude, life purpose, understanding and engagement (VALUE) all influence how they will respond to the flow of the coaching sessions.

A coach brings their expertise and knowledge to 'hold' their clients, work with them, keep their VALUE and goals in focus, and provide the best possible coaching environment for the coachee to benefit from.

Although the process and success of the coaching process are not based on the coach having the same experiences in life as the coachee, it is inevitable that a relationship built on a rapport and 'sameness' will be easier and quicker to establish. The challenge for the coach is they do not bring their own experience and resolutions into the coaching process. If this is needed, then the relationship is either a mentoring or consulting one and needs to be acknowledged as such.

The challenge for the coachee is not to seek out a coach with a similar personality so that they can feel comfortable and safe. They need to choose a coach who will champion, challenge and create trust in a way that allows the coachee to stretch and test themself and learn. If the sessions start to feel like comforting moments in the diary rather than learning experiences, then both the coach and the coachee will need to decide if they are working together in the best way.

COACHING HOMEWORK

Reviewing your clients, how are they reacting to the peaks and plateaus of the coaching process?

What happens in your own coaching during times of peaks and plateaus in the coaching process?

CLOSURE

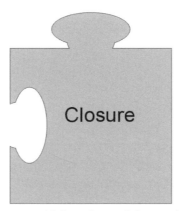

Fig. 26.   Closure – 4th key phase of the coaching process.

Closure is the 4th phase of the coaching process.

There are two aspects to the process of closure.

1. Completing the coaching session
2. Concluding the coaching relationship.

COMPLETING THE COACHING SESSION

One of the biggest concerns for coaches is the thorny problem of knowing how to conclude a coaching session when the client is in the middle of important 'stuff'. For example, the coachee has had an insight and would like to work through it before they lose their train of thought, they are telling the coach of a bad debt their business has just incurred, or they have just heard their about a family issue such as their mother needing ongoing medical care. It makes no difference whether the coaching takes place face to face or over the telephone. When the session is coming to an end, clients need to take themselves and the session experience back to their life and the coach has to move on to their next appointment.

It is at times like this that the coach needs to remember that their client is 'naturally creative, resourceful and whole'. Even if there are loose ends at the end of the session, the client is more than capable of handling the uncertainty. It is up to the coach to articulate what is going on, and offer support to the client. For example:

Coachee: '*You know I've just had a sudden thought that I keep making these situations more complicated – when I think I'm keeping it simple for everyone – hey how dumb can I be?*'

Coach: '*Great insight you've just had – it feels very clear and important to coach around further. Sadly I see we are getting to the end of the session, so I'd like to leave you with an inquiry. No quick answers – just some to reflect on. So . . . How would it be like if everyone kept it simple for you? See where that takes you and send me an email of your reflections before our next session.*'

The coach has articulated what is happening, acknowledged the importance of the client's insight and left the client with an inquiry to work with so the learning is not lost. Finally the coach has offered support in the form of a structure to email any thoughts the client has around the inquiry. In this example, lots of different coaching skills are being used together in the service of the coachee.

Supporting from a distance

The coach needs to remember that the client is responsible and accountable for their own actions and is more than capable of making sense and resolving any untidy ends that might occur at the end of a session. The coach's responsibility is to remind the client that they are supported, and to do so in a way that is of maximum benefit to their clients. If the coach does not feel their client is capable, then that is a good indication that the coach is not viewing the client as a whole person and needs to ask if coaching is right for the client at this time.

There are several different actions that coaches use, depending on their own style, to conclude the session. Some coaches keep a record of the session and the coachee's homework for the next session for their own use. Other coaches email summarised notes of the session (including homework) to their client, other coaches keep no notes believing it is the responsibility of the client to action what they need without the coach keeping track of them.

Most coaches, in all areas and niches of coaching, offer contact between sessions to review progress or to celebrate a success. None of these models and styles are confined to just 'life' coaching or 'executive' coaching. Every coach uses their own style to carry out and close a coaching session.

COACHING HOMEWORK

What are you willing to offer your clients, to conclude the sessions and keep contact alive between sessions if needed?

CONCLUDING THE COACHING RELATIONSHIP

At the end of the coaching programme (whether the client feels that they have completed all they need to achieve or the time limit of the coaching commissioned is at an end) the coach and coachee need to formally conclude the relationship.

This can range from reviewing the metrics of measurement designed for the coaching (see page 149) to agreeing that a break is needed in the coaching process and booking a future check-in date in future months to re-examine the circumstances of the coachee.

It is always a useful exercise for the completion process to ask the coachee for feedback of the coaching experience. For example:

♦ What was useful for you when being coached?

♦ Could anything have made the coaching process more beneficial for you?

♦ What would you like to acknowledge, and congratulate, yourself for having experienced or leant?

♦ Is there anything else you need or would like to say before we conclude this last session?

AFTER-CARE SERVICE

When the coaching sessions have concluded, most coaches do not think of it as the end of the relationship. Most coaches actively create an 'after-care' service, through which the coachee knows they can still make contact in the future if they want to check-in or need a sounding board, at no extra cost to the them. Usually, this continued level of contact is available to all clients, whether they paid for the coaching themselves or were sponsored.

COACHING HOMEWORK

What will you do to conclude the coaching for your clients?

IN SUMMARY

♦ Use the insights and information gathered in the springboard session to energise the ongoing coaching process.

♦ Allow the coachee to learn and experience the coaching in their own time and personal styles.

♦ Use all the coachee's spoken and unspoken action to help inform developments in the coaching process.

♦ Regularly review progress with the coachee so they can learn from failure as well as successes and re-calibrate actions where needed.

♦ Let the coachee know the coach is beside them at all times, and not just during booked appointments.

5
Third Party or Sponsored Coaching Programmes

The practice of coaching started in sports, then moved into the business world following the publication of Tim Galloway's *Inner Game* books on golf and tennis, and then later entered the world of work. The premise of Galloway's research and writings came from his curiosity about why, despite having the same technical skills and talents, some people could perform better in the game of golf or tennis. What made the difference, apart from the obvious reasons such as bad weather, or attending a party the night before or similar such reasons? Also – and in spite of any of these excuses – could a person still be able to perform at their full potential?

Many of the people who then played golf and tennis were successful business people, so it did not take long for them to ask themselves the same questions about their own potential and performance in the workplace – and that of their teams. Coaching is an accepted part of modern workplaces and has proved time and again that it does make a difference in the success and profitability of organisations, especially during times of bad economic climates and in the face of increasing competition.

This chapter will review and illustrate the practice and factors that ensure a successful and fully utilised use of coaching in the workplace, from the line manager to HR's use of internal coaching through to contracting an external coach. Issues discussed include:

- Who is the client – the coachee or the company?

- How to ensure the confidentiality, expectations and success of the coaching delivered.

- Understanding the lines of responsibility, accountability and authority of coaching managers and internal and external coaches.

- Setting up the coaching programme as a form of continuous professional development and knowledge management, within the organisation.

DEFINING THE MANAGER AND THE INTERNAL COACHING ROLE

Coaching within organisations can be delivered by a number of different people: by managers coaching their teams, both as groups and one-to-one; by the Human Resources (HR) staff, where coaching is part of their responsibility across the organisation; and finally, by external independent coachees who may work on special projects and often for more senior members of the organisation.

The coaching delivered by managers can be both informal and formal. Informal coaching is based on ad hoc meetings – and may not even be at a pre-arranged meeting, but based on a manager's 'open door policy' for his team and his leadership style. Some organisations and managers require that one-to-one meetings for all team members are held on a regular basis. These can cover specific learning and development needs, or they could be a way of allowing managers and team members to keep in individual contact and resolve any issues that may arise in workplace projects. Such issues may include managing their own teams, or performance issues, or completing their own department's aims and objectives.

Proactive organisations will have a training programme that managers can attend to learn how to use soft skills, as well as hard business skills, for their own managerial development. Managers will then learn how to use these soft skills in a coaching manner, for conflict resolution, supervision and the mentoring of junior staff (and in some professions, to help them gain chartered status). Coaching skills can also be used within groups and across departments for special projects, such as product design and innovation between the research and development (R&D) department and the marketing and sales team, as well as for interdepartmental knowledge. The setting up of co-coaching projects can also give a leading edge for companies against their competitors. To get the best out of these sessions, there needs to be a formal coaching programme so that goals are set, the foundations and ground rules amongst the group are established, and the different styles and attitudes of everyone are taken into account. In essence, the group, team or individuals co-coaching each other will need to set up the coaching using the four key phases of the coaching process shown in Figure 7, page 23.

'Internal coach' is the term usually given to a member of the HR department whose responsibility it is to coach individuals within the workplace. They may also facilitate the coaching by managers or project leaders of teams and groups if needed, may train members of staff in soft skills and their use and may even supervise the coaching techniques of their own co-workers and managers. These programmes can be run both formally and informally. Often organisations have coaching clinics that members of staff can drop in to if they need to, or some are run in the same way as employee assistance schemes through using the telephone and out sourced HR professionals. Internal coaches need to have been professionally trained in coaching skills, must belong to a coaching professional body, and should be committed to on-going CPD and regular supervision just in the same way as an external professional coach would be.

USING INTERNAL AND EXTERNAL PROFESSIONAL COACHES

One of the frequently asked questions in business is whether to have internal coaches, or to outsource the function, or to have a combination of the two. One independent coach attended a business breakfast at which the speaker, from a global financial firm, shared with the audience their best practice of employee development at all levels. This included offering a comprehensive coaching programme for employee support and learning. Later that day, the coach met a young manager from the same firm. As he spoke about the concerns he had of managing a global team that was part of his new responsibilities, the coach mentioned the presentation she had heard earlier in the day about the coaching and support offered by his firm.

Coach: *Since there is a company coaching programme specially designed to support employees and a keen commitment to managerial development, have you taken part in an in-house programme?*

Coachee: *Are you kidding? If you go and ask for coaching it is seen as a weakness, and the HR department that controls it records it all on your employee records. If your manager sends you then it is perceived you must be well below par and not up to the job. So I can only really go to my boss, but since he is part of my new concern who is there that will be totally safe and confidential?*

This is not an unusual response. Whether it is true or not, HR departments generally do have problems convincing employees that they are genuine in following the ethics of confidentiality. Sadly, it is not unknown that external coaches have been asked by members of HR or line managers for an update or report on confidential coaching sessions. Another 'complaint' by senior managers is that internal coaches are usually of a more junior level or pay grade to them, so they often do not feel the internal coach is experienced enough to coach them. The more truthful reason is that as senior managers they simply do not want to be seen to have to ask for support. They will also forget that the practice of coaching is really about people dynamics and not sector knowledge. Coaching skills are used across all types of industries and organisations. Each coach is an expert on the skills that will enable others to become more self-aware and realise their own potential. It is coachees in turn who will have the industry knowledge required to make organisations work.

There is still a strongly upheld myth in many organisations that the more senior you are, the more you should know without the support or input of others. This is an outdated piece of reasoning and often denied, but sadly it still exists and is perpetuated by leaders in all sectors. For such people, the danger is that if they request support and reflection, it will be from others like themselves who will collude with their existing behaviour and points of view. It is true that internal coaches can experience issues of conflict. They are employed by an organisation and therefore it is difficult to question decisions. Whereas an external coach can leave a project if they strongly object to an issue or behaviour, it is not so easy for an internal coach. They are on the staff and it might mean losing a permanent job.

The most successful senior teams and organisations know that reflection time, keeping an open mind and asking for others input encourage innovation, creativity and high performance. The process of coaching works well enabling and encouraging these behaviours and attitudes.

The external coach has an additional advantage in that they are not tied into the culture or organisational politics. They are simply contracted to do a job and then leave. They are in a position to be able to ask the difficult questions, highlight the time wasting or disrupting behaviours and to hold a mirror up so an organisation can see itself as others do. Contracting external coaches is also a cost effective way of having access to expertise without the overhead costs of employment. In addition, external coaches can be beneficial during times of change and transition and in difficult situations. The 'stranger on the train' scenario does bring out a high level of truth and honesty, which provides the bedrock for sustainable and co-operative transformation. It would be more helpful for organisational behaviour if senior executives were to be open about encouraging the work of coaches that they have experience of. If nothing else, they could be honest about both the positive and negative experiences that are part of the responsibility of senior promotion. One external coach had to submit their invoices for personal payment by the Managing Director, so the accounts department and HR would not know that some of the board were being coached.

ISSUES OF ACCOUNTABILITY, RESPONSIBILITY AND AUTHORITY

Depending on who is coaching whom (internal or external coaches, line managers or co-coaching) this will influence the various approaches to accountability, responsibility and authority that govern the nature of the relationship between a coach and coachee. Professional coaches set up formal coaching relationships based solely on the needs and agenda of their clients. Managers, however, will have definite agendas that will be interlinked with the individual success of their own performances.

For example, if a coach is the line manager of a coachee, there will come a point where the manager will be directive about actions and goals. While they may not have a strong preference as to how a project is completed, they will need to have certain goals achieved. The manager may also want the coachee to learn certain elements and practices in the workplace for professional development that the coachee is not interested in, and in order to gain the training needed to achieve this, the manager, as coach, will be directive about the process irrespective of their coachee's willingness. The main influences that drive achievement are organisational aims and objectives, not personal goals and motivation.

The balance of accountability, responsibility and authority of internal coaches is different. The coach may be attached to a HR department and will train and mentor managers on their skills for managing teams and performance as well as coaching staff. They will therefore have a double agenda. One for the employee as their coachee, and another which is duty to the company. Non-executive directors (NED) hold a similar double-sided agenda. Their position on the Board means, as stated in the Higgs Review of guidelines for Non-Executives (NEDs) published in 2003, that they are balancing holding an independent, non-directive role for the executive board and yet have a directive responsibility for the strategic direction of the organisation.

Within the voluntary sector there are both paid officers and volunteers working together and sharing responsibilities for the effectiveness of the organisation. Depending on the relationship and motivation of the coach and coachee it would be easier to use a directive style with paid officers to accomplish goals, rather than with volunteers who need to be engaged in their performance and motivated to give their time and expertise free and therefore are usually happy for backing with a non-directive, supportive style. There will be occasions when internal coaches within organisations, however much they try, will have issues with being totally non-directive in a coaching relationship. They have a duty to their employer and their own employee performance to maintain. See Figure 3.

Professional coaches will have spent many hundreds of hours of supervised training and will have committed themselves to continual professional development (CPD) and regular supervision. A coach working at this level only uses a non-directive style and is usually external to the organisation or in no way connected to the coachee. The coaching agenda and aims will be the client's – the coachee – and must not be influenced by the coach. If the coach feels that there is an issue with the coaching relationship they can end it immediately.

The hierarchy of position and power a coach might have over the coachee also affects the balance of accountability and responsibility that is expected within the relationship.

CONFIDENTIALITY AND EXPECTATIONS WITHIN ORGANISATIONS

Confidentiality is the cornerstone of any coaching relationship. As discussed earlier in this chapter, rightly or wrongly, this is a difficult point sometimes for organisations to guarantee. The practice of establishing a 'safe and courageous coaching space' is fully discussed in Chapter 3, pages 80–3, and is followed by the co-designing and logistics of the coaching relationship. These practices need to be followed whether the coaching is sponsored or directly paid for by the coachee.

Part of the initial meetings and springboard sessions between the commissioning manager and the coachee will need to openly discuss and plan how these can be achieved to ensure a successful and effective coaching process for all the parties included: the manager who is sponsoring the programme and their agenda; the team member who will become the coachee and will therefore be subject to the same degrees of autonomy and confidentiality as those who pay for their own coaching; and the coach who wants to work within an ethical and professional framework. Here the coach has a duty to deliver a professional service to the paying sponsor, but also an ethical and professional duty to the sponsored coachee.

HOW TO PREPARE AND RUN AN ORGANISATIONAL COACHING PROGRAMME

The request

All coaching starts with the request. The coach will need to know who made the request and why. If there is an open coaching programme then the coachee will be the one to come directly to the coach and explain their reasons. Many corporate open programmes have to be signed off by a manager, in which case they will have an agenda as to why they are sanctioning the expenditure. For example, is this coaching partly a request by the leadership or professional development, or an issue of under performance? It may be that a manager has directly requested a team member to be coached. In cases like this there will need to be a pre-springboard session with the manager concerned. This could take place with or without the coachee being present. Whatever happens, the coach will need to be open with the coachee so they know which areas and goals of coaching they wish to see achieved.

Accepting the organisational boundaries

Most large organisations will have a preferred supplier list, so the boundaries of coaching services for external coaches will already be established and accepted. There have been cases where coaches have declined to work in organisations because they have felt the prearranged programme is too short or inflexible, or has been set up in such a way that it ticks a HR compliance box. It is important to know the way an organisation or sponsor is willing to support the coaching. Often this is based on a financial decision alone.

COACHING HOMEWORK

Ask yourself the question: 'Does the way the coaching programme has been set up suit you?'

Establishing the ground rules and boundaries

Every organisation is different. Maybe a coach has reached a point when they have one preferred way of working? It will be healthier if a meeting is arranged with the relevant line manager. This helps to establish some ground rules around issues such as confidentiality, and sets the boundaries of expectations while agreeing on certain logistics like the time period of the programme, the number of sessions, where and how they are to take place. The coach can thus share their ethics and standards and understand those of the organisation. This meeting also gives a chance for the manager to state what they want for this team member and for the coach to understand how the manager will know this has been achieved. This is an important process in establishing how success can be measured qualitively and quantively. On some occasions the manager will have this meeting with the coach, and it is up to them to relay the information to the coachee. If the meeting can include the coachee, then it should create a greater understanding between all three people involved.

LOGISTICS

It may sound simple, but many a sponsored coaching programme has failed because there was no quiet, confidential location to meet face to face or to speak on the telephone. Tensions will have been created because a coachee has had to make the calls from home in their own time, or because a coach has realised that they are having to cover unexpected expenses to make sure the sessions are not overshadowed because there is a physical and psychological barrier. With coaching in general, coaches need to be clear about the way they work with coachees. Even where coaching is being paid for by a third party, it is always the coachee that the coach must establish a rapport with for a successful and effective outcome.

A SPRINGBOARD SESSION FOR A SPONSORED COACHEE

The first meeting between a coach and coachee on their own the agenda needs to be explored in the same way as that with any other client, so they can discover their own goals and issues and work out if there are any conflicts of interest. For example, an external coach should be able to openly balance the two agendas in the coaching session. They can work with the coachee to build on their confidence and decision-making processes to satisfy the manager, and also work on other issues should the coachee have to leave the company and find another job. Internal coaches however can be faced with a significant issue of conflict. They will have no problem working with the manager's agenda, but they may well feel uncomfortable when dealing with coaching issues based on the coachee wanting to change jobs, unless the manager is happy to let his team member move on. In cases like this, the experienced internal coach will explore the issues of why the coachee wishes to leave, and what they may need to do to improve any of the current conditions, behaviours or attitudes that are pushing the coachee to leave. It is surprising the number of times clients want to change their employer, only to find through coaching sessions that if they change some of their own behaviours and attitudes the situation improves.

INDIVIDUAL, TEAM AND GROUP COACHING

Corporate or sponsored individuals

Coaching corporate or sponsored individuals needs to be set up following the same process as laid out in Chapters 3 and 4 (*Creating the foundation of the coaching process and The coaching process*). There may be a need to change some of the language to suit the culture and sector jargon if this creates a more meaningful language.

Group and team coaching

In a corporate setting there are many obvious opportunities for coaching groups or teams:

♦ Knowledge management

♦ Motivating staff – especially during times of change and transition

♦ Problem solving

♦ Building trust across an organisation

♦ Resolving conflicts

♦ Reflection and planning of business aims and objectives

♦ Employee, or volunteer, learning and development

♦ Creating and sustaining a team

♦ Appraisals and fact finding staff surveys.

There are many reasons here. What is important is that the coaching process, whether one-to-one or in a group, allows the opportunity to communicate ideas, get feedback and enable people to work at their best.

There are two different ways that groups come to together for coaching:

1. A group of people who join a group for coaching with unrelated agendas
2. A group (or team) with a common purpose or aim.

A group of people who join a group for coaching with unrelated agendas

Creating a group for coaching, whether by telephone or face to face, is a good way to offer low cost coaching. Sometimes a group may form themselves and ask the coach to work with them for a period of time. Some coaches offer group coaching as one of the ways to be coached by them.

The dynamics of the group are that each coachee has an allotted time to be coached directly in front of the group, and in between sessions, the whole group is available to co-coach each other. The coach still requests that the coachees in the group all complete and send the coaching prep form to the coach before each session. In some cases coaching prep forms are circulated throughout the group as a whole.

The coach is also available for contact and support between sessions for the individual coachees if required.

The group may have very different agendas and areas where they want support, or they could all be connected by a similar theme, for instance, they are all starting their business, or are women working in a traditionally male profession, wanting to live abroad or write a book. Each vision and end goal does not include any other member of the coaching group, yet they have similar considerations. Everyone in the group will learn from each other's experiences and insights to further their own development.

A group or team with a common purpose or aim

This group may come together as an existing or newly formed team. Their common purpose and agenda has a relevance to each other, even if they are coming from differing backgrounds or experience. Team coaching is often sponsored by a third party so there needs to be clarity about boundaries and confidentiality within the group and the sponsoring party.

Group coaching is often arranged as a combination of group and individual coaching – the coachees bring together their own personal needs or professional development for the benefit of the common agendas and goals. The team comes together to formulate the focus of the group and how they will interact with each other between sessions. As an addition to the group coaching, individuals in the group are often coached separately for their own development, to be able to participate in the team coaching to a high level.

CONCLUDING THE COACHING RELATIONSHIP

A sponsored coaching programme will usually have a built-in cut off point that both the coach and coachee will work towards. In coaching programmes with private coachees, there will be an agreement to review the process at certain points. However, this may not be possible and many external coaches will have had the frustration of coachees wishing to continue but not being able to find the funds to pay for this, either personally or through the company. It is a difficult decision for coaches to make sometimes. One coach stated that she always allows personal clients free access to her via the phone if they needed a quick sounding board or were updating their news and achievements. This coach also said that she was always prepared to give one free session if it were needed to wind up the programme and that she always offered such coachees the same aftercare service she gave her paying clients. Other coaches, however, will step away from coaching programmes if they find they are not able to give coachees an open and supportive coaching experience.

COACHING HOMEWORK

Have you any conditions under which you will not carry out sponsored coaching contracts?

SETTING UP A MENTORING PROGRAMME FOR SUSTAINABLE PROFESSIONAL DEVELOPMENT

Internal coaches and managers who are expected to work within a coaching ethos will need to have an ongoing support and development of these skills. A few quick hours or days, even if over a period of some months do not make managers proficient in coaching skills. This is a valuable role that internal coaches can play – to be on hand to give refresher skills sessions or to listen and coach a manager through any coaching issues they may have. External coaches can be a great resource in supervising, both for internal coaches' skills and for managers to keep on the ball with a process that may play an important part in their responsibilities, but this is not generally a huge part of their role. One global company worked out that coaching should only take 5% of manager's time, and yet they were expected to be able to make up that time on a regular basis and to a high standard. With all the other professional pressures exerted on managers, they admitted that team coaching had become an irregular activity due to last minute cancellations both by managers and teams.

MEASUREMENT OF SUCCESS

Part of the process of closure is for both the coach and coachee to review the measurement stated at the beginning of the process. Usually this is a recurrent activity and part of the learning and experience to check if there needs to be any recalibration of goals. Measurement is discussed again in Chapter 6 (pages 167-8). Organisations like to talk about measurements as rates of investments (ROI), so it is well worth a coach stating at the beginning of the coaching process with the manager that the ROI will continue after the coaching programme has finished and that they would like to contact them and assess the ongoing ROI, 6 and 12 months later (see some of the following examples).

The entrepreneur
Setting up a clinical research outsourcing business, based on the ethics of improving drug availability and costs to developing countries.

Agreed measurement:

♦ To part of the development of a 2 billion dollar sector of clinical research and outsourcing trials in Asia and the developing world.

♦ Company 5 year target of £10 million.

♦ Personal vision to bring health and revenue to India.

♦ Have first research trials in India, using alliances created by end of first year.

Qualitative:

♦ Personal satisfaction of starting up a CRS company based on ethical values.

♦ Acknowledged by both the competition and prospective clients as having sound business acumen and a recognition of unique personal background, expertise and integrity.

♦ Great personal satisfaction in being offered this new position by a client that gives her greater global standing and raises her game and honours her personal values.

♦ Personal recognition of the need to be interactive within a big organisation at this point in her career.

Quantitative:

♦ Financial – buy out of business before end of first year's trading, equity in existing company and financial stability.

♦ Future bonus/reward revenues for 5 year period.

The organisation

The original brief was to coach a team of senior executives. Following the initial coaching sessions and further discussions with the HR director, an executive director and CEO highlighted a more fundamental problem.

First phase coaching – initial foundation coaching sessions with managers.
Second phase coaching – *Taking the Temperature*™ coaching style survey of 40 senior managers.
Third Phase coaching – continue to coach 14 senior managers.

Agreed measurement:

♦ Staff retention – to ensure that by improving managers' morale the company retained its key managers at a vital time of change.

♦ To rebuild trust between managers and Board – meaningful manager meetings.

Qualitative:

♦ To enable the CEO to understand what the managers valued in the relationship.

♦ To re-establish the regular meaningful managers' meetings – with a full disclosure of information.

♦ Over time, to discuss and implement recommendations for the report.

♦ To re-create lost trust and retain key members of staff, raising morale and team performance.

♦ To discover unknown and unutilised talents and skills within staff in the organisation.

Quantitive:

The coaching process enabled the company's culture to transcend organisational barriers and to turn the focus on distrustful non-cooperation towards a free flow of highly profitable and rewarding bottom-line business. For example:

♦ All the 14 senior managers who were coached remained within the organisation.

♦ One existing profit centre went within 12 months from a revenue of £1.5 million to £5 million bringing in a return of 270% from the external coaching fee for the project.

♦ Other new global profit centres were utilised following the identification, development and support of the entrepreneurial spirit of managers.

Return on Investment

Coaching is cost effective for organisations because it is an on-going relationship encompassing review, assessment, and refined goals, that consolidates and keeps clients focused.

IN SUMMARY

♦ Know the client and how to ensure the confidentiality, expectations and success of the coaching delivered.

♦ Be aware of the differing lines of responsibility, accountability and authority of coaching managers and internal and external coaches.

♦ Set up coaching, supported by a supervision programme as a form of continuous professional development and knowledge management, within the organisation.

♦ Always respect the culture and attitudes of the sponsor, even if the coach and coachee will be actively challenging them as a result of the coaching sessions.

♦ Encourage continuous lifelong learning as a normal business and professional activity.

6
Setting Yourself Up As A Coach

Your coaching practice is yours to design and run in any way that suits you. Maybe you started coaching to enable you to have balance and more control in your working life, or are working full-time as a coach and need to generate a sizeable income to meet your needs. Whatever the reasons you became a coach, your requirements and your desires need to be met by the coaching practice you create. This chapter also reviews working practices which are equally applicable for those who work as internal coaches in the workplace or offer skills to the voluntary sector.

The late Thomas Leonard, who set up the training school *CoachU* and later *Coachville* expressed the opinion that it was only when a coach had 'put his arms around' his 100th client, that he would understand what coaching was about and who he was as a coach.

FINDING YOUR COACHING STYLE

All coaches are different and there are many styles and models of coaching available. There is no such solution as a 'one size fits all' magic coat of coaching that will ensure success. Creating a coaching business is not for the faint hearted. Being employed as an internal coach in the workplace is very different from running your own coaching business. However, there are similar concerns like creating ethics, standards, organisational terms and conditions, internal charging, measurement and confidentiality boundaries for the coaching process.

Coaches come from all backgrounds and experience, and as a result bring many different elements to support the coaching process. Although these elements may include services and products from a past business experience, it is important to be able to distinguish the coaching elements apart from the 'add on' income generating products that align well in a coaching business. For example, psychometric and diagnostic tools such as Myers Briggs or DISC based systems.

Phil Sandahl, co-author of *Co-Active Coaching* said 'On the whole the world was not looking for coaching in the same way as it is not looking for six inch drill bits. However, the world is looking to make six inch holes and therefore needs six inch drill bits in the same way as they are looking for a fuller, more purposeful and enjoyable life which are the benefits of coaching'.

This chapter reviews the:

♦ Five easy steps to a sustainable and profitable coaching business

♦ Coaching groups and teams

♦ Tips and traps of coaching

♦ Frequently asked questions about coaching

♦ Setting ethics, standards, terms and conditions

♦ Forms and toolkit for coaching.

FIVE EASY STEPS TO A SUSTAINABLE AND PROFITABLE COACHING BUSINESS

1. Be a trained and accredited coach
2. Be professional
3. Identify customers and create awareness
4. Networking and professional contacts
5. Professional fees.

When setting up a coaching practice you need to think of running it as a successful business even if you started to coach from a choice and a way of life. Follow the five easy steps to sustaining a profitable coaching business:

Be a trained and accredited coach

Being able to present recognisable coaching qualifications and continuous professional development (CPD) shows your commitment to the profession. There are many different coaches training organisations. The professional training bodies listed in 'Resources' show the training organisations that they accredit and this is probably the best way of deciding where and how to continue your professional coaching development on a regular basis while you are offering coaching services.

Be a professional

The professional coaching body that you chose to align yourself to will probably have access to services and information you will need to establish yourself as a business professional. Points to consider include: subscribing to data protection and having a professional indemnity policy. You should also investigate whether you need to be a sole trader or a limited company and be VAT registered. Decisions may depend on who your customers are and what their expectations are for suppliers. Make sure that your business cards and stationary looks professional. Many coaches base their business from home but have a business address for all contact and a specific business phone line. Some coaches have an additional separate line for incoming telephone coaching calls only.

Identify your customers and create awareness of your service

Do you have specific clients that you would like to coach? Is there a special niche of coaching you would like to create? Will you offer group coaching as well as coaching individuals? Do you prefer to coach by telephone or face to face, or will you offer a combination of both?

Do you need a printed brochure or will you have a web presence? When you have answers to these questions then you can formulate a marketing and public relations strategy to raise awareness.

Have a network of referrals and professional contacts

Which kind of networking associations would you like to be a part of? Which of the associations are your clients members of? In what kinds of situations are you most enrolling as a professional? How and where do you enjoy meeting people most? Coaching is a service that creates business through building relationships and personal referrals rather than advertising and cold calling. However you decide to create new networks and use existing ones, there needs to be a constant flow of new business.

Charge a professional fee

If you are a professional you need to charge a professional fee. There are coaches who run special discounted schemes for clients they would like to coach, who cannot afford their fee. Some coaches even commit to having one or more pro bono clients at any one time. They choose to do this as their way of giving to the community and not because they do not know how to charge a professional fee. To be unclear about your fees and to be fearful of properly charging for your services undermines the skills and the professionalism that you have.

To help focus time and energy between providing coaching and working on running a business, there are ten habits that will help you track the time you spend – or not – each month. The ten areas are:

1. Client coaching
2. After-care and general client contact
3. Marketing

4. Public Relations
5. Accounts/administration
6. Continual Professional Development (CPD)
7. Contribution to Coaching Community
8. Scheduled reading time: trade/professional journals
9. Networking and updating professional connections
10. Other.

The coach's toolkit enables you to track and analyse the total hours you spend each month on these activities, details of the activity and the result. In time you will be able to see how successful certain activities are and create a balance of your energies between working in your business and on your business.

Income streams

Associated products are another area in which to look for further income streams that complement a coaching business i.e. amazon.com for books you recommend, psychometric assessments, diagnostic tools and specific training programmes that you may be trained to deliver or create an association with an expert who specialises in these areas. These are not offered as 'coaching' but as complimentary areas for coaching to be allied to or followed up.

As a new business there are local and national government schemes that can help you. For example, your local business link who can help you with any accounting, legal and financial queries you have and highlight any local grants and assistance for which your new business is eligible. There are a number of business agencies listed in Resources (page 186).

COACHING HOMEWORK

What are your goals for your business?

How can your business be most aligned with your values and vision as a coach?

Coaching is a service – do you want to offer additional products to your clients?

TIPS AND TRAPS OF COACHING

The coaching relationship is a co-created, designed alliance that ensures a collaborative coaching process between the coach and coachee. The coach uses their training and experience to know when to use, and which to use, of their skills, techniques and talents for the maximum benefit of their clients. During the coaching relationship it is important for the coach to be fully aware of the traps that can appear to disrupt the flow of the process and tips to counteract the energy and imbalance that can result.

Signs of client dependency

There are four distinct signs that a coachee is becoming dependent on the coach. A coachee may begin to seek advice, rather that wanting support to gain insights, and ask the coach what they should do.

1) **No thoughts** – The coachee nearly always asks for the answers rather than working through a problem and coming up with a solution themselves.

2) **No confidence** – The coachee has a tendency to ask the coach to do things for them, rather than making decisions and taking concerted action.

3) **No foresight** – The coachee misses insights and opportunities through a lack of foresight or an inability to see the whole picture.

4) **No initiative** – The coachee tries to rely on the coach to get things going rather than risk making mistakes and failing in the task themselves.

Tackling dependency

At any sign of dependency, the coach needs to highlight what they are seeing and coach around the underlying issues. Maybe the client is not ready and there is an issue that needs to be referred to another professional. It could be that the client is not committed to the coaching process at this time, or that they need to have a break from the regular coaching sessions to tie up loose ends at work or home before they can truly commit to coaching. Maybe, just being their coach and naming what you see will give them all the insight they need to re-calibrate and clarify the next steps they need to take in the coaching process. You are the professional coach – so you will know how best to 'hold' the interests of your client. Do not forget to take this issue to your supervisor. If you can get the coachee's permission to record the session – better still for the supervisor to listen to the session 'live'.

100 per cent client attention

As a coach you need to be strong and assertive about the boundaries you decide to set as a professional to conduct your coaching sessions. Clients can forget that a coaching session is not merely a helpful, encouraging, supportive conversation. A lot of left and right brain activity is required and they need to give a hundred per cent of their concentration, awareness and thought processes to the session.

It is very tempting for busy, organised and expert multi-taskers to try and slip coaching calls in amongst other activities. It is equally important that the coach is not heard rustling through the kitchen making cups of coffee and trying to tap quietly on their computer while listening on their hands free phone to their clients.

Coaching is always in the best interests of the client

A coach needs to develop a sense of when the client is ducking and diving, and when it is beneficial to end the session early. One new coach found her client was definitely stretched to the limit and not 'present' in the call. The coach decided in the first minute of the call that the client was not involved, and having heard the explanation of the client's day the coach wondered how she could suggest that this call could be closed. It took her 29 minutes of a 40 minutes session to finally state the obvious and end the call, arranging that the client email or telephone the next day just to check-in.

For the whole of the 29 minutes the client was wondering how they could end the call too and not feel weak or sound uninterested in the coaching. Sometimes the most valuable thing a coach can do for their clients is to state what they see in the session and give the client the opportunity to do what is best for them without feeling that they have failed to achieve something and move forward.

Getting swamped in the day-to-day activities

It is the responsibility of the coach to be able to balance the day-to-day 'stuff' that the client highlights in the sessions, with the chosen goals, primary focus and broader vision that the client has for their own life. It is very easy for the coachee to get bogged down with the day-to-day stuff of life, and for the coach to collude in this problem solving with ongoing, practical sorting of niggles and issues in the coaching sessions. In the end, the coach is just facilitating the client to fire fight situations, rather than looking at cause and effects. The coach needs to be able to raise the client's head out of the morass of the moment.

To 'do' and to 'be'

For many clients, it is easier to 'do' than to 'be'. In fact for some the very word 'be' is too airy-fairy for them and sounds spooky and alternative in an unacceptable way. As a coach you need to be able to support your client in understanding that, for example, the state of 'doing' is a state of 'being' busy. Another example is that by making that difficult phone call – 'doing' – they were 'being' courageous or forgiving or courteous to make it.

To 'be' all the time is a daydream and to 'do' all the time is a nightmare. The coach needs to support the client in creating a consciousness of having both states in their life for a balance that benefits them. As a coach you need to have this balance in your life too so that you can signpost the way and flow for your clients.

Can't go there

There are occasions when, as a coach, you 'can't go there' for your client. The coachee could be saying, acting or touching a subject that you are not comfortable with. If that happens, as their coach you need to either tell your client and deal with the situation accordingly (if it is their agenda) or note the situation down and contact your mentor coach or supervisor as soon as possible (if the agenda is personal to you).

An experienced coach called her supervisor to discuss a long-standing client.

Coach: *Every time I tell him that I will be away for two months over the summer and that I am not coaching any clients he becomes either a little victim being abandoned, or uses it as a way to try and emotionally blackmail me by saying he won't be able to concentrate on completing the manuscript if I am not around to coach him. I know none of this is true, but I am feeling unable to cope with it as it is reminding me of my old behaviour of helping everyone, even to* *my own detriment. Somehow I can't go there to discuss it in some assertive, productive way. This is not so much about a sudden dependency on my client's side, but more a fact that I don't seem able to deal with it.*

A professional coach is someone who is very honest about themselves. Working with people is a rewarding, and testing way of life. Self-awareness, self-care and management are essential for the coach – and never being too afraid to ask someone else for help.

OOPS – Over Operational Planning Syndrome

The process of planning, agreeing future actions, structures and expectations makes an energetic, exciting, dynamic process for clients. When everything seems to be going well, clients can get to a stage when they are loading themselves up with much more to do than they can handle, or try rushing from one stage to the next without pausing for reflection.

For some clients, self-esteem is confirmed simply by them successfully achieving their expectations. A client may lose self-esteem if they willingly offer the coach long lists of 'things to do' that are impossible to complete by the next session, or if they have totally underestimated the work they need to carry out. The motivation and energy that comes from newfound clarity, insight and achievement begins to disappear under the pile of 'intended – but didn't get done'.

It is a case of OOPS – named by John Vercelli, one of CTI's earlier leaders *'over operational planning syndrome'* which is de-motivating and disheartening. The coach needs to be aware of when this is happening and point it out to the client. It may be part of the client's development to experience overload and learn from it. The coach is there to support and facilitate the client in any way that creates the best coaching environment.

WAIT – Why Am I Talking?

Coaches need to be careful that they are allowing the coachee to do the talking and not themselves. There are some clients that seem to absorb anything the coach says like a sponge. The coach needs to be aware of the interactions during the session and ask themselves:

♦ Why am I talking and not the coachee?

♦ What effect is my talking having on the coachee?

♦ Am I colluding to overstepping or missing something important here because I am talking and not listening?

♦ What am I trying to say? Do I need to bottom line what I am saying here?

FREQUENTLY ASKED QUESTIONS ABOUT COACHNG

The most frequently asked questions from clients tend to cover five main areas:

1. Time

'How much time is this going to take?'

For many clients, time is at a premium. There are many different combinations of coaching sessions and programmes available. Coaching frameworks range from telephone coaching once a week for half an hour to meeting clients face to face for two to three hours once a month, with a half an hour catch-up call in between each coaching appointment.

Coaches decide how they are going to work with their clients depending on their own needs and working styles. Some coaches only practice telephone coaching and others will only work with clients face to face. There are coaches that only plan to work the first three weeks of a calendar month which allows them a fourth week to concentrate on their business and enables them to take time off without disrupting their clients' schedules.

It is not unusual for coaches to insist on a defined period of coaching commitment from their clients on their terms and conditions. The most usual is a three month commitment from the client for personal coaching and written notice of 30 days for the termination of the coaching contract.

2. Fees
'What is it going to cost?'

Coaching fees range from pro bono clients to some executive coaches charging FTSE 100 companies tens of thousands of pounds for each corporate coachee which is sponsored by the company.

As a coach you will need to decide what your level of fees are. There are several approaches to deciding these scales:

♦ Find out what the competition is charging and react accordingly by charging less or by charging more.

♦ Decide how much you need to earn and base your fees on your personal needs.

♦ Design a service for your niche clients and charge a level of fees that is acceptable to them and generates a higher volume of income.

Each coach needs to set their own level of fees, terms and conditions for coaching. As a coach you need to be clear about your fees structure and be willing to refer prospective clients to other coaches if your fee structure does not suit them.

3. What is coaching?

'What happens in a coaching session?'

This question covers two aspects of coaching. Although the question appears to be asking how the coaching is run, the real enquiry is what is coaching compared to other better known forms of professional support such as therapy, mentoring and consultancy. These points are fully discussed in the Introduction, however the clearest answer for the prospective client is that coaching is a professional service that helps people to discover and reach their goals and supports them in any way that aids their learning and actions for the future. The premise of coaching is that all coachees are naturally creative, resourceful and whole, and therefore they are clients and not patients. Coaches do not give advice and their sole aim is to support their client's agenda in any way that is of maximum benefit.

4. Coach's experience

'What is your background – how did you come to coach?'

Professional coaches come from all backgrounds and experience and for many different reasons. For some prospective clients it is very important to them that their coach has some knowledge of their background or profession. However, coaching is about personal dynamics and not a sector specific profession.

5. Coaching benefits

'Is what I want okay for coaching?'

Coaching is a relatively new profession so there are many prospective clients who do not clearly understand what the benefits are from coaching other than that they have heard it recommended. There are many different reasons that clients come to coaching – ranging from life changing decisions to achieving a work/life balance. The coach needs to know what issues and situations they are confident to coach in and where their boundaries are in relation to referring clients on. Only the coach knows whether the issues presented by a prospective client are ones they are happy to coach on.

However, for the client's benefit it is often useful to be able to share with them some of the benefits of coaching. These include motivating and encouraging, challenging and supporting, reflecting and experimenting in a relationship that is totally confidential, safe and non-judgemental, where the client's agenda is paramount.

MEASUREMENT OF COACHING

It is often said that coaching is difficult to measure. In some cases, the results are intangible, therefore not easy to measure in the traditional sense of hardcore facts and figures. However, when all clients come to coaching, the first question coaches ask is 'What do you want from coaching?' Other questions that help to clarify the expectations and goals of the coachee are 'How will you know when you have it?' 'What will it look like?' The client's answers will all give indications of the end goal. These are the measurements that have value for the coach. Quantitive and qualitive measurements are equally important

Personal measurement

To find points of reference to measure the personal impact of coaching, an easy and simple place to look is the Wheel of Life that the client completed in the springboard session (see Chapter 3). This is a record of the circumstances of their life when they start coaching and by the coach asking how to bring those marks up to a full rate of 10 (see Figure 27, page 171) will give an insight into the kind of measurement that is important to the client.

As all clients are different, the points of measurement do not have to be logical or rational to anyone else, as long as they are meaningful to them. One client may want to move jobs to work in a career that helps them provide for their expanding family and create more balance in their lives by paying others to do the day-to-day chores. Other clients might want to bring more balance into their life by downsizing. Another client may need an annual physical challenge and break their routine of the desk job and convenience of the urban life, versus a client who wants to spend a sabbatical in Africa working with children of refugees as an embodiment of a personal value.

Organisational measurement

Coaching in the corporate and organisational world needs to have some form of tangible measurement. There have been two informative reports on places to look for measurement within organisations and surveys to record the hardcore impact in statistics and percentages. These are, *Impact Evaluation Report on the Coaching.com Intervention* and *The Return on Investment of Executive Coaching* (see Bibliography and Further Reading).

When any organisation commissions coaching, the coach needs to ask what they are trying to achieve and how they will know when it has been achieved. It may be a clear goal. For example a charity might say they would like to pass on a higher percentage of the money they raise for their cause by lessening the administration costs. They could have calculated it is possible to achieve their goal if they could retain more volunteers for a longer period to cut down on time spent training new volunteers. These aims begin to create a measurable framework for the coaching process, and allow for additional benefits to be discovered while coaching the individuals and groups within an organisation.

In the same way, a commercial organisation, may want to increase productivity and relations with its staff after a reorganisation. For example, one company identified key employees to be considered essential to inbedding the new re-structuring. The coach will need to draw out areas of measurement that are of value to the client, for the organisation as a whole and the personal measurements for the individuals coached. For more examples of measurement in 3rd party coaching programmes see Chapter 5.

SETTING ETHICS, STANDARDS, TERMS AND CONDITIONS

Ethics and standards

The best place to start creating your own set of ethics and standards is to align yourself with those that your coaching professional body will uphold. However, it is necessary that you take ownership and responsibility for creating any additional ethics and standards that you feel are important to illustrate your values as a coach and cover situations that arise as you become more experienced in your coaching practice. The fundamental views of a coach (on their professionalism, standards and ethics) rarely change from the beginning of their coaching career. However, increasing experience over time gives coaches a greater insight into areas of ethical decisions and dilemmas that were not obvious when they started coaching. These may include a greater sensitivity to cultural and social differences or a realisation of your impact in certain areas. As with continuous professional development, your ethics and standards need to be regularly reviewed.

COACHING HOMEWORK

The following questions will help you to start to discover and create your personal professional coaching ethics and standards:

What are the stated ethics and standards of your professional coaching body?

What are the ethics and standards you want to include beyond those laid down by your professional body?

You could answer these Coaching Homework questions in relation to the following issues:

♦ Conditions of confidentiality

♦ Responsibility and accountability as coach

♦ What can you guarantee from coaching?

♦ What can you not guarantee from coaching?

♦ What are your coaching boundaries and how would these affect your clients?

♦ Conflicts of interest

♦ Ethical violations.

Terms and conditions

The terms and conditions document that you produce can be as simple or as complicated as you like. There are companies who prefer you to base your contract on generic organisational contracts, but for your individual clients the contract you ask them to sign can be designed in any way that suits you and your coaching practice.

The simplest terms and conditions contract will cover:

♦ Fee structure

♦ Payment methods

♦ Logistics of coaching sessions

♦ Contact details for coaching sessions

♦ Any special conditions.

However, there are additional situations that arise during coaching relationships and these need to be covered in your terms and conditions document. Here are some additional points to consider:

♦ missed appointments

♦ cancellation

♦ missed payments

♦ emergencies

♦ commitment period of coaching

♦ measurements for coaching outcomes

♦ special conditions requested by client.

FORMS AND TOOLKIT FOR COACHING

Checklist for toolkit and forms:

For coach's use

• Terms and conditions – coaching contract

• Debit/credit card processing information

• Client's personal details

• Client checklist and coaching record

• Client springboard session information.

For client's use

♦ Client's goals – resources, planning, support structure

♦ Wheel of Life

- Financial statement

- Money management

- Daily habits to form balanced and fulfilled life

- Coaching session prep form.

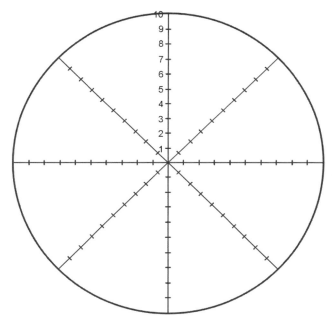

Fig. 27.   Wheel template.

For coaching business

- Your personal resource list

- Ten business habits for the month of . . .

- Sample referral letter.

Sample Terms and Conditions

Fee: The fee per calendar month based on (face to face/telephone coaching)
Coaching session is £ .... (including VAT)

How to pay:
1. By cheque (payable to ....) and sent to
....
2. Credit/debit card – XX, YY, ZZ – please find credit/debit card details form enclosed.
3. By standing order. The payment needs to be received by the 1st of each month ahead. To pay by standing order my bank details are as follows:
Bank/address ....
Sort code ....
A/c name ....
A/c number ....

Payments: Payments are due on the 1st of the month unless otherwise agreed. I don't permit late payments, unless prior arrangements have been made. It is the responsibility of you, the client, to keep me informed of any changes in circumstances that may cause payments to be missed or delayed. I reserve the right to suspend or terminate the coaching contract should there be an ongoing issue of payments.

I will provide a receipted invoice once payment has been received.

Coaching sessions: Our agreement includes (...) x coaching sessions per months which will be (by telephone/face to face). Each coaching session is for up to (... length of time) unless otherwise stated.
Telephone coaching sessions: Please call me at ..../Face to face meeting: please meet me at ....

Changes: If you need to reschedule your session, please give me at least 48 hours notice. If you have an emergency (illness) we will work around it, otherwise a missed call cannot be made up. If I need to change a scheduled call I will also give at least 48 hours notice except in an emergency.

Page 1

Extra: You may call/email/fax me between your calls if you need advice, support or can't wait to share a success or have a problem.

Problems: If I say or do something that upsets you or doesn't feel right, please bring it up. I promise to do whatever I can to sort it out.

Our coaching relationship is confidential. To be clear about the professional standard and guidelines of coaching, please read the 'Ethical Guidelines' enclosed and then complete the rest of the form on the following pages. Please sign and return both pages to me.

Signed: Date:

Printed name:

Page 2

Sample
Credit and Debit Card Processing Information

.... is hereby authorised to charge monthly to the following credit or debit card the amount shown for Personal and Business Coaching or other program as noted below, until terminated in writing. Upon completion, please either fax or return the original to your coach, keeping a copy for your own records. Thank you.

Credit and Debit Card Information

Client name: ....

Client telephone number: ....

Billing address: ....

....

Name on Credit or Debit card: ....

Expiry date: ....

Issue No: ....

Amount: ....

Please circle one: Card X   Card Y   Card Z

Authorised signature: Date:

Client's Personal Details

Personal Information Factsheet
All personal information is confidential and treated appropriately.

Client Information
Full name ....
Name you like to be called ....
Home address ....
Work address ....

Telephone Numbers
Home telephone ....
Work telephone ....
Pager ....
Fax number ....   Email address ....

Occupation
Employer name ....

Other Personal Information i.e. Dates/Family etc.
Date of birth ....
Marital status .... Number of children ....
Significant other's name ....
Significant others D.O.B. ....
Wedding/special anniversary date ....
Name(s) and age(s) of child(ren) ....

Sample
Client Checklist and Coaching Record

Name

	Date			
Terms and Conditions		❏ Email	❏ Post	❏ Fax
Ethics and Standards		❏ Email	❏ Post	❏ Fax
Coaching pre form		❏ Email	❏ Post	❏ Fax

Springboard		Outcome
Month 1		
Session 1 Session 2 Session 3 Session 4		
Month 2		
Session 1 Session 2 Session 3 Session 4		
Month 3		
Session 1 Session 2 Session 3 Session 4		

Springboard Session Information

Five Viewpoints of Future Life

V – Values ....

....

A – Attitude ....

....

L – Life Purpose ....

....

U – Understanding ....

....

E – Engagement ....

....

Goals and Primary Focus for Coaching Programme

1 ....

2 ....

3 ....

Coaching Relationship

How do you want your coach to be? ....

Barriers/structures/help for coaching process ....

Logistics

Coaching Forms Checklist   *Date*

Terms and Conditions

Payment Details

Ethics and Standards

Coaching Prep. Form

Goals – Resources, Planning, Support Structure

GOAL No. ....

SMART goal check

S – specific ....
M – measurable ....
A – achievable ....
R – realistic ....
T – time-tied ....

People

Have ....
Need ....
Sup. Struct ....

Places

Have ....
Need ....
Sup. Struct ....

Other Factors

Have ....
Need ....
Sup. Struct ....

ACTION PLAN   *Stages Completed*
1. ....
2. ....
3. ....
4. ....
5. ....

Financial Statement

Assets   *Debts*

Assets		Debts	
Cash in hand	_____	Overdraft	_____
Current acct. balance	_____	Credit card balances	_____
Savings acct.	_____	Loans – business/pers.	_____
Pension	_____	Mortgage outstanding	_____
Insurance	_____	Finance/credit agreements	_____
Stocks/shares	_____		
Life assurance	_____	Current bills	_____
Property	_____	Tax owed	_____
Jewellery	_____	Other	_____
Furniture	_____		
Care etc.	_____		
Arts/consumables	_____		
Clothing	_____		
Elec. equipment	_____		
Money owed	_____		
Other	_____		
	_____		_____

Assets – Debt = Net Worth

Net Worth =

Money Management

Tracking Your Financial Habits

Below is a sample list of spending categories. (Taken from *How to Get Out of Debt and Live Prosperously* (1990) by Jerrold Mundis)

Tracking down your financial habits is a process. Over a six-week period write down everything you spend your money on, from 40p on a newspaper to monthly mortgage payments, using the categories suggested below. At the end of each week add up your list of expenditures in their categories and then in total. This process informs you of your actual spending habits and values and serves as a map for future decision-making.

- Alimony
- Books
- Car (petrol, tyres, insurance, maintenance and repair
- Charitable contributions
- Children's expenses
- Clothes
- Café/Snacks
- Council Tax
- Debt/Loan repayments
- Entertainment
- Entertainment/others (paid for others)
- Gas/electricity
- Gifts/others
- Gifts/me
- Groceries
- Hair/beauty
- Health club
- Hobby/recreation
- Holidays/travel
- Home equipment (television, radio, dishes, pots, pans, appliances, tools

- Home furnishings (tables, chairs, beds, rugs, drapes)
- Home heating
- Home repair/maintenance
- Home insurance
- Home supplies/cleaning
- Income taxes
- Investment/pension
- Magazines/newspapers
- Medical
- Miscellaneous (under £10)
- Personal growth
- Public transport
- Rent/mortgage
- Telephone
- Taxis
- Toiletries
- Others

Daily Habits to form a Balanced and Fulfilled Life

Under each heading your client needs to list what daily habits and regular actions are needed to create their unique balanced life.

Health

....

....

Romance/significant other

....

....

Physical environment

....

....

Money

....

....

Personal learning and growth

....

....

Fun and recreation

....

....

Career

....

....

Family and friends

....

....

**Sample
Coaching Session Preparation Form**

Get the most out of your coaching sessions by preparing for them. Either return a completed copy of this form, by fax, or use the questions her to send me an email 24 hrs before your next coaching appointment.

1. What have I accomplished since our last session?

2. What didn't I get done, but intended to?

3. What challenges and problems am I facing now?

4. What are the opportunities which are available to me right now?

5. What are the great insights I've had during the period?

6. For what do I feel grateful for right now?

7. How do I want to use the coach during the call?

8. What do I agree/promise to do by the next call?

9. Anything else?

Your Personal Coaching Resources List

For referrals and signposting: Specialist Coaches, Other Professionals, i.e. Legal, Accountants, Health etc.

Name	Profession	Contact details
1.		
2.		
3.		
4.		
5.		
6.		
7.		
8.		
9.		
10.		
11.		
12.		
13.		
14.		
15.		
16.		
17.		
18.		
19.		
20.		

Ten Business Habits for the Month of _____			
	Total hours	Activity	Result
1. Client coaching			
2. After-care and general client contact			
3. Marketing			
4. Public Relations			
5. Accounts/administration			
6. Continual Professional Development			
7. Contribution to Coaching Community			
8. Schedule reading time: Trade/professional journals			
9. Networking and updating professional connections			
10. Other			

Sample Referral Letter

Coaches Name

Qualifications

Address

Name and Address of

Referred Professional   Date

Dear . . .

Veronique contacted me, having been referred by an old client. She wanted to start coaching to change her working life, which may affect her personal circumstances by involving a move from London.

Veronique and her partner both work in stressful jobs in the City and have come to the realisation that there has to be a better way to live. They have tried to make decisions in the past on their future together, but sadly they get swamped in the pressures of life. Veronique has been to see her doctor (name) for stress-related illness and her partner has admitted that he has a problem with anger. The main reason for the timing of her contact to me was that they had an argument the night before which had resulted in her partner agreeing that they seek support.

Having spoken to Veronique, I have told her that, while I am happy to coach her on career matters, to gain the maximum value of coaching I felt that she would first need to resolve some more personal issues around her relationship with her partner. I suggested that they are counselled, as a couple, since all problems I heard in their relationship have been present and unresolved for some time.

I have suggested to Veronique that she contacts her doctor again to seek his advice and given her your contact details as a therapist who is experienced in these matters. I have agreed to send a copy of this letter to Veronique and have arranged that she contacts me to update me on her progress.

Thank you for your help in this matter. If you have any queries, please do not hesitate to contact me.

Yours sincerely

[signature]

Resources

Professional Bodies

Association for Coaching www.associationforcoaching.com/

European Mentoring and Coaching Council
    www.emccouncil.org/

International Association of Coaches
    www.certifiedcoach.org

International Coach Federation www.coachfederation.org/

Training and Development

Supervision and coach mentoring

Email: supervision@proactivecoaching.com

For accredited Continued Professional Development (CPD):

1) Refer to above listed professional bodies for their accredited programmes.

2) Refer to UK universities for affiliated coaching programmes. For example:

The School of Coaching Programme,

affiliated to University of Strathclyde,
    www.theworkfoundation.com/solutions/soc/ind ex.htm

Software

Client Compass www.Clientcompass.com

ACT! 6.0 Organises Your Business www.amazon.co.uk

Coach Track www.Coach-Track.com

On-line coaching community
www.eurocoachlist.com/

Business
Data Protection Act email: data@notification.demon.co.uk
Helpline: 01625 545740
Business Link – managed by the DTI. Tel: 0845 600 9 006
    www.businesslink.gov.uk/
UK Government Grants Directory. www.grantsonline.org.uk
The British Chambers of Commerce. Tel: 020 7654 5800 Email: info@
    britishchambers.org.uk
TelecomsAdvice – for small UK businesses who need to know about
    using telecoms and the Internet.
    www.telecomsadvice.org.uk/
Companies House Tel: 0870 33 33 636
Email: enquiries@companies-house.gov.uk
    www.companieshouse.gov.uk/
Federation of Small Businesses Tel: 01253 336000
    www.fsb.co.uk

Referrals and Signposting

Addiction and Support
Al-Anon Family Groups UK and Eire
61 Great Dover Street
London SE1 4YF
Tel: (020) 7403 0888
Email: alanonuk@aol.com
Website: www.al-anonuk.org.uk
Provides support for family, friends and colleagues of alcoholics.

Alcoholics Anonymous
PO Box 1
Stonebow House
Stonebow
York YO1 7NJ
Tel: 01904 644026
Website: http://www.alcoholics-anonymous.org.uk
Offers advice and support for alcoholics.

Gamblers Anonymous (UK)
PO Box 88
London SW10 OEU
Tel: (020) 7384 3040
Website: http://www.gamblersanonymous.org.uk/
Provides support for people with gambling problems.

Narcotics Anonymous (UK)
202 City Road
London EC1V 2PH
Tel: (020) 7251 4007 (for literature)
Email: ukso@ukna.org
Website: http://www.ukna.org
Provides support for people with drug problems.

Sex Addicts Anonymous: details of meetings in the UK
http://www.sexaa.org/meetings.htm

Adoption Services
British Agencies for Adoption and Fostering (BAAF)
Skyline House
200 Union Street
London SE1 OLX
Tel: (020) 7593 2000
Email: mail@baaf.org.uk

Website: http://www.baaf.org.uk

BAAF is the leading organisation for agencies and individuals concerned with adoption.

Office of National Statistics: Adopted Children Register
Adoptions Section
General Register Office
Smedley Hydr,
Trafalgar Road
Southport PR8 2HH
Tel: (0151) 471 4830
Email: adoptions@ons.gov.uk
Website: http://www.statistics.gov.uk/nsbase/registration/
adoptions.asp

The Adopted Children Register is kept by the Registrar General and contains a record of every person who has been adopted through a court in England or Wales.

Post Adoption Centre
5 Torriano Mews
Torriano Avenue
London NW5 2RZ
Tel: (020) 7284 0555
Advice line: (020) 7485 2931
Email: advice@postadoptioncentre.org.uk

Counselling and Psychotherapy
British Association of Sexual Relationship Therapists (BASRT)
PO Box 13686
London SW20 92H
Email: info@basrt.org.uk
Website: http://www.basmt.org.uk

Cruse Bereavement Care
Cruse House
126 Sheen Road
Richmond
Surrey TW9 1UR
Tel: (020) 8940 9530
Helpline: 0870 167 1677
Website: www.crusebereavementcare.org.uk
Offers help and counselling for bereaved people.

Health
The ME Association
4 Top Angel
Buckingham Industrial Park
Buckingham MK18 1TH
Tel: (01280) 816115
Website: http://www.meassociation.org.uk
Provides support and information for those affected by ME, Chronic
    Fatigue and Post-Viral Fatigue Syndrome.

Lone Parent Services
Families Need Fathers
134 Curtain Road
London EC2A 3AR
Tel: (020) 7613 5060
Email: fnf@fnf.org.uk
Website: http://www.fnf.org.uk
Provides information and support to parents of both sexes.

Gingerbread
7 Sovereign Close
Sovereign Court
London E1W 3HW
Tel: (020) 7488 9300

Advice line: 0800 018 4318
Email: office@gingerbread.org.uk
Website: http://www.gingerbread.org.uk
Provides information about support for lone parent families.

Retreats
The Retreat Association
The Central Hall
256 Bermondsey Street
London SE1 3UJ
Tel: (020) 7357 7736
Email: info@retreats.org.uk

Burrswood
A Christian Hospital and Place of Healing
Groombridge, Tunbridge Wells
Kent TN3 9PY
Tel: 01892 863637
Fax: 01892 863623
Email: enquiries@burrswood.org.uk
Website: www.burrswood.org.uk

Senior Citizens
Age Concern England
Astral House
1268 London Road
London SW16 4ER
Tel: (020) 8765 7200
Information line: 0800 009966
Email: InfoDep@ace.org.uk
Website: http://www.ageconcern.org.uk
Offers information on issues such as money, legal topics, health, community care, housing, transport, heating, leisure and education.

Help the Aged
Head Office
207–221 Pentonville Road
London N1 9UZ
Tel: (020) 7278 1114
Email: info@helptheagd.org.uk
SeniorLine: for FREE welfare rights advice, call 0808 800 6565
Website: http://www.helptheaged.org.uk
Provides services for the elderly to live independently, particularly
   those who are frail, isolated or poor.

Glossary

Acknowledging

A coach needs to acknowledge the client during their process of learning, taking actions and developing within coaching. This is a way of pointing out the client's talents that they may have forgotten, or celebrating a recent effort they have been making to change a behaviour or learn a new skill, however successful they have been. It is about acknowledging the client's effort and energy to accomplish their aim.

Articulating

The coach needs to articulate what is going on for the client, and make sense out of the client's story. Sometimes being honest and just asking the question, 'Hold on a moment, I am not quite sure I understand what you are trying to say' gives the client an indication that there are discrepancies or oddities in the coaching session that need to be examined more closely. By articulating, the coach shows the client the effect of what they have been saying and telling the coach and therefore the outside world.

Asking permission

For the coach to truly hold the focus and gain depth in the coaching, there will undoubtedly be times when subjects are broached or issues raised when the client is feeling defensive or resistant. By the coach asking permission, the client knows that this is being done with their best interests at heart. Whatever the outcome of the discussion, the coach is showing respect to the client by asking permission to 'go there'.

Bottom lining

When a client is deep in the story, however poetic, colourful or interesting it may be, it is the responsibility of the coach to know when to say, 'Hold on a moment. What are you really trying to get at? Can you bottom line that for me?' Bottom lining is about giving the essence of the story, or the strapline of the situation.

Challenging

Challenging is an extension of requesting. Sometimes it is referred to as a mega request. The idea of the challenge is that the coach chooses something that they know the client will feel is way beyond them, a real stretch. The client has a choice of saying 'Yes', 'No' or counter offer.

Championing

Championing enables the coach to bring to their client's attention what they are capable of and how this will benefit others. It is a way in which a coach can support the actions and efforts of their client.

Clearing

Clearing is a way of dealing with anger, frustration or negativity that gets in the way of the coaching. The coach agrees a limited time – say five minutes – for the client to moan, groan and wallow and holler in the aggravation of the situation to get it out of their system. When the time is up, the coaching recommences leaving the negativity behind.

Corporate or business coaching

The specific remit of a corporate coach is to focus on supporting an employee, either as an individual, as part of a team and/or organisation to achieve improved business performance and operational effectiveness.

Dancing in the moment

As with any kind of collaboration the coach and client must be able to explore all avenues and perspectives as they present themselves. The skill for the coach is to be able to work with the client and take these moments of insights and diversions in the coaching session by 'dancing in the moment' with the client and yet never losing sight of the client's agenda. The inspiration and insights come from the flexibility that the coach is able to give during the coaching sessions to explore all avenues and yet not lose sight of the main focus.

Executive coaching

Executive coaching is specifically focused at senior management level. The coach and coachee explore business related topics as well as personal development topics in order to improve their personal performance.

Geography

A coach needs to recognise the effect of the client's physical geography, stance, tone of voice and pace of speech or their current mood and how to change it for the client's benefit. For instance, if a client is recounting a situation in a sad, monotone voice and they are explaining that they are tired and unable to achieve anything the client needs to be able to change that tone of voice either by themselves, lightening their own voice and pointing out the geography in the tone of the voice of the client. Whether you are coaching face to face or over the telephone there are clues for the coach to understand the attitude of mind and emotional state of the client.

Group coaching

Group coaching is working with a number of individuals either to achieve a common goal within the group, or create an environment where individuals can co-coach each other.

Hold the grand purpose

At all times the coach needs to be able to hold the client's greater purpose in life through all the day-to-day living and unexpected demands. Very often clients have failed in the past to live the life they truly want and to contribute in a way they wish to because they get bogged down in day-to-day life and the grander purpose has been lost sight of and been forgotten.

Inquiry

Inquiry is a form of questioning that the coach employs to open up the thinking and believing processes of the client. An inquiry is an open-ended question and is not to be answered immediately. It is a thought provoking inquiry for the client to view certain aspects and situations.

Intruding

It is part of the coach's job to point out and challenge any issues that they see their client avoiding. A coach needs to learn the skill of intruding and taking charge when they feel their client telling long, involved stories or digressing within the coaching conversation in order to avoid a difficulty.

Intuition

Intuition is a gut feeling or flashes of unrelated thoughts that come into the mind and have a feeling of truth and possibility attached to them. Although intuition has the overtones of something 'spooky', third sight or just plain creepy, it is fascinating to note the number of times a seemingly off the wall thought or mental picture by the coach is a perfect illustration of what is going on for the client that they have been unable to fully express.

Meaningful language

Meaningful relationships naturally form their own communication shorthand that enables access to clear understanding. This is created and built up throughout the coaching relationship, starting in the springboard sessions, creating a unique shorthand for the client's values, purpose, visions and meaning of their life.

Meta/helicopter view

The meta/helicopter view is an objective view that frees up the client's thinking and experience of situations by taking a view from above. This enables the coachee and coach to view the situation from a broader vision by looking down or from a helicopter view.

Mirroring

The skill of mirroring works in two ways: 1) That at times the coach is physically holding up a mirror for the client so they can perceive how they are being seen by others and 2) The coach copies or mirrors the client's physical stance, movements, tone of voice and language as a way of creating empathy and connection with the client.

Non-verbal communication

There are many ways in which information and meanings can be expressed without words. There has been much research undertaken on the meaning of body language but it is part of the human makeup to automatically understand aggressive or friendly body language without knowing the full extent of the subject. The pace, pitch and tone of the voice is a great indicator of emotion and intention. Sometimes non-verbal communications is known as 'observant listening'.

Open/closed questions

Closed questions tend to be able to answered with a YES or NO. They do not open up, or lead on the thinking while answering the question. For example:

'Is this an effective strategy for you?'

To ask this as an open question would inspire creative thinking thereby giving a fully and more considered answer:

'What makes this an effective strategy for you?'

Pacing

Pacing forms a bridge of rapport with others through interactional synchrony. It is a way of harmonising and engaging in action that is complementary to the other person. For example, a coach might match the enthusiastic or curious frame of mind of their client to engage in the coaching process.

Personal/life coaching

Personal/life coaching is a collaborative solution-focused, results-orientated process in which the coach facilitates the enhancement of work and life experiences and any other areas from the coachee's personal agenda.

Powerful questions

What makes a question powerful is starting it with the word 'What' rather than 'Who, Why, When or How'. The 'What' questions forces you to be specific in your enquiry which leads to specific solutions and awareness. For example, if you ask 'Why are you reading this book?' your client will tend to give a story as an answer. If you were to ask, 'What outcome do you want to reach by reading this book?' the answer is future-orientated and focuses on insights and solutions.

Re-calibrating

Being to able to review current experiences and re-calibrate actions and attitudes needed for a more positive outcome is the fourth stage in the learning process. In a similar way that a coach helps the client re-frame thoughts and perspectives on situations, the coach also helps the client gain more perspective and choices from the experiences they are having by being able to assess and if necessary re-calibrate actions for the future.

Re-framing

The skill of re-framing is to help the client consider their language and thought process in a different way. For example, if the client is feeling hard done by in a particular situation they are thinking about the situation from the limiting standpoint, that life is like a glass half empty. The coach needs to ask the client to look at the same situation in a different way, to re-frame the situation and can ask a powerful question 'What would the situation be like if you were grateful for what you have now?'

Requesting

When a coach is making a request of a client they are asking them to commit to achieve something which the coach hears the client wanting or needing to do but not settling down to it. For example, the coachee may need to contact some customers. The coach will request that they do contact them between the coaching sessions instead of hearing during continuous sessions how the client has not had the time – but must – contact customers. Requesting encourages the client to focus on an action and to carry it out. By the coach requesting these actions they are asking commitment from the client to achieve them. The client has the opportunity of saying, 'Yes' 'No' or counter offer.

Responsibility and accountability

There is responsibility and accountability for both the coach and the client during the coaching process. The coach needs to ask if there are any special areas of responsibility and accountability that the client would like them to hold for example, not to over plan or over commit to actions or to make sure they follow through and complete actions before moving on to the next. It is the coach's responsibility to sustain a safe and confidential coaching environment, to be the best coach they can possibly be, and the client is responsible and accountable for their own learning and actions during the coaching process.

Speciality/niche coaching

Speciality/niche coaching is usually undertaken by coaches knowledgeable at addressing a particular aspect of a person's life, for example career or creativity, or is focused on a particular section of the population, for example, doctors or youths.

Structures

Structures are ways in which the client and coach have agreed to keep action and learning on track. For instance, the client may decide to keep a journal throughout the coaching process as a structure to gain insights and learning from the process in between coaching sessions. If a client needs to make a difficult phone call the coach can offer the structure that the client contact them before making the call and after. Other structures can include visual aids like photographs, postcards or collages that have a specific meaning to the client.

VAK

Visual, Audio, Kinesthetic (VAK) is a mode of language and understanding that clients naturally prefer to use in all forms of their communication and choice of langauge.

Visual – 'I see what you mean'
Auditory – 'I hear what you mean'
Kinesthetic – 'I sense what you mean'

When we think about something we enclode our 'thoughts' using our 'senses'. Everyone tends to be stronger in one or other of the VAK modes.

Bibliography and Further Reading

Alder, H (2001) NLP: *The New Art and Science of Getting What You Want*, Piatkus Books, London.

Anderson, Dr. Merrill C, *The Return on Investment of Executive Coaching*, Metrix Global LLC, www.metrixglobal.net

The Arbinger Institute (2002) *Leadership and Self-Deception*, Berrett-Koehler Publishers, San Francisco.

Block, P (1981) *Flawless Consulting*, Jossey-Bass Pfeiffer, San Francisco.

Bono, J E, Purvanova, R K and Towler, A J (2004) *Executive Summary for Coaching Survey*, Technical Report CR04180, University of Minnesota.

Buzan, T (1991) *Use Both Sides of Your Brain*, Atlantic Books.

Buzan, T (2004) *How to Mind Map*, HarperCollins, London.

Cameron, J (1995) *The Artist's Way, A Course in Discovering and Recovering Your Creative Self*, Macmillan Publishers Ltd. London.

Carroll, M and Gilbert, M C (2006) *On Being a Supervisee: Creating Partnerships*, CIPD.

Carson, R D (1990) *Taming Your Gremlin, A Guide to Enjoying Yourself*, Harper Perennial, New York.

Cava, R (1999) D*ealing with Difficult People*, Piatkus Books, London.

Cook, L (2000) *Working Mum: The Survival Guide*, Simon & Schuster UK Ltd, London.

Cope, M (2003) *Personal Networking*, Pearson Education Limited, London.

Covey, S R (1994) *The Seven Habits Of Highly Effective People*, Simon & Schuster Limited, London.

De Shazer, S (1994) *Words Were Originally Magic*, New York, Norton & Co.

Fairley, S G and Stout, C E (2004) *Getting Started in Personal and Executive Coaching*, John Wiley & Sons, Inc.

Forrest, A (1995) *Fifty Ways to Personal Development*, The Industrial Society, London.

Forster, M (2000) *Get Everything Done and Still Have Time to Play*, Hodder & Stoughton, London.

Fortgang, L (1999) *Take Yourself to the Top*, HarperCollins, London.

Gallwey, T (1974) *The Inner Game of Tennis*, Random House, New York.

Gallwey, T (1981) *The Inner Game of Golf*, Jonathan Cape, London.

Gallwey, T (2001) *The Inner Game of Work*, Random House Trade.

Gigerenzer, G (2002) *Reckoning with Risk*, Allen Lane, The Penguin Press, London.

Givens, D B (2004) *The Nonverbal Dictionary of Gestures, Signs and Body Language Cues, From Adam's-Apple- Jump to Zygomatic Smile*, Spokane, Washington: Center for Nonverbal Studies Press, http://members.aol.com/nonverbal2/diction1.htm

Goleman, D (1996) *Emotional Intelligence, Why It Can Matter More Than IQ*, Bloomsbury Publishing Plc, London.

Goleman, D (1998) *Working with Emotional Intelligence*, Bloomsbury Publishing Plc, London.

Goleman, D (2002) *The New Leaders, Transforming The Art Of Leadership Into The Science of Results*, Little Brown, London.

Hammond, S A (1998) *The Thin Book of Appreciative Inquiry*, Thin Book Publishing Co, USA www.thinbook.com

Hawkins, P and Shohet, R (2000) *Supervision in the Helping Professions* (Open University Press).

Hay, J (1993) *Working it Out at Work: Understanding attitudes and building relationships*, Sherwood Publishing, Watford.

Hayden, C J (1999) *Get Clients Now!* Amacom.

Honey, P and Mumford, A (1983) *Using Your Learning Styles*, Peter Honey Publications, Maidenhead.

Jacobs, M (ed.) (1996) *In Search of Supervision*, Open University Press.

Jeffers, S (1991) *Feel the Fear and Do It Anyway*, Arrow Books Limited, London.

Jeffers, S (2003) *Embracing Uncertainty*, St. Martin's Press, New York.

Kay, F, Guinness, H and Stevens, N (2003) *Making Management Simple*, How To Books Ltd, Oxford.

Kay, F ((2003) *Kickstart Your Time Management*, Capstone Publishing Limited, Oxford.

Ken Blanchard Companies, (2001) *Impact Evaluation Report on the Coaching.com Intervention For [Client Company]*, www.coaching.com

Kidwell and Lee (Eds) (2006) *Managing Organizational Deviance*, Sage Publishing, USA.

Kline, N (1998) *Time to Think: Listening To Ignite The Human Mind*, Cassell Illustrated, London.

Kolb, D and Fry, R (1975) *Learning Circle of Experience*, McBer and Co, Boston.

Kuiper, J A and Dance, K A (1994) 'Dysfunctional attitudes, roles, stress evaluations, and psychological well-being', *Journal of Research in Personality*, 28 (2).

McMeekin, G (2000) *The 12 Secrets of Highly Creative Women*, Conari Press, Berkeley, California.

Mole, J (2003) *Mind Your Manners – Managing business cultures*, 3rd edn, Nicholas Brealey Publishing, London.

Munchhausen, M von (2005) *The Little Sabateur*, Cyan/Campus Books, London.

Mundis, J (1990) *How to Get Out of Debt, Stay Out of Debt and Live Prosperously*, Bantam Books, New York.

Mundis, J (1996) *Earn What You Deserve*, Bantam Books, New York.

O'Connor, J and Seymour, J (1994) *Training with NLP: Skills for Managers, Trainers and Communicators*, Thorsons, London.

O'Connor, J and Seymour, J (1995) *Introducing NLP: Psychological Skills for Understanding and Influencing People*, The Aquarian Press, London.

Pease, A (1984) *Body Language: How to read others' thoughts by their gestures*, Sheldon Press, London.

Prior, D M, MCC, MBA, Co-Chair, ICF Ethics and Standards Committee (2003) *Professional Coaching Language for Greater Public Understanding*, www.coachfederation.org

Smith, H W, (2001) *What Matters Most, The Power of Living Your Values*, Simon & Schuster, London.

Stevens, N (2007) *Mentoring – A Powerful Tool for Women*, Woman@Work No 7, EuropeanPWN publication www.EuropeanPWN.net

Sutton, J and Stewart, W (2002) *Learning to Counsel*, How To Books Ltd, Oxford.

Whitmore, J (1997) *Coaching for Performance*, 2nd edn, Nicholas Brealey, London.

Whitmore, J (1987) *The Winning Mind*, Fernhurst Books, Steyning.

Whitworth, L, Kimsey-House, H and Sandahl, P (1998) *Co-active Coaching: New Skills for Coaching People towards Success in Work and Life*, Palo Alto, CA, Davies-Black.

Yeung, R (2003) *Coaching People: Develop and motivate your team to achieve great results*, How To Books Ltd, Oxford.

Zohar, D and Marshall, I, (2001) *Spiritual Intelligence: The Ultimate Intelligence*, Bloomsbury Publishing Plc, London.

Reviews

I found *Learning to Coach* to be a very user-friendly book to read. Easy to understand and to the point, it gives a great introduction and overview to the practice of coaching used in the professional and personal development arena. An excellent place to start.

Prof Bruce Lloyd
Strategic Management, London South Bank University

The buyers of coaching services

Nicola Stevens book *Learning to Coach*, apart from demystifying her subject and pointing to the value and skill of the coach in both the personal and professional arena, achieves something far more important. At a time when everyone seems to know how too coach or is being coached, she has benchmarked potential clients for us, and how to identify the true professional coach from the well meaning amateur.

Martyn Hurd
President of BKSTS – The Moving Image Society & Treasurer and Council Member of Broadcast Journalism Training Council (BJTC)

Learning to Coach hits the bull's eye – at last clarity for those wanting to use coaching and benchmarking for professional coaches. Nicola Stevens understands the hard core concept of measurement and value in the world of business, as well as creating meaningful worthwhile experience for the individuals concerned.

It put me on the right road to understanding coaching. *Learning to Coach* answers the questions that need to be asked to gain value from the coaching process and make the money and time well spent.

Gareth Robertson
MD WCPR Ltd
Financial Publishing Co

Index

acknowledging and championing, 39, 41, 133
aftercare, 83, 133
agendas
  big A, 106–8, 160–1
  clients, 106–8, 160
  little a, 107–8, 160–1
articulating, 39–40
asking permission, 25, 28
attention
  client, 159–60
attitudes, 78, 88–92

balance
  creating, 89–90, 106–8
  priorities, 92
barriers
  coaching process, 96–9
  learning, 100
'be', 161
bibliography, 201–4
bottom lining, 39–40, 194
boundaries, 53, 79, 82, 143
  checklist, 70
brainstorming, 33, 36–7
business coaching, 194

challenging, 46–7
clearing, 29, 31–2
client's agenda, 14
client's own qualities and style, 112, Fig. 20
closure, 23, 108, 130, 134
closure relationship, 132–4
closure session, 131–2
coaching
  background, 1
  business, 154–5
  core competencies, 21–2
  definition, 2–6
  for coaches, 15, 96–7, 186–7
  groups and teams, 145–7
  methods, 15
  managers, 136–7
  models, 108–12
  qualities, 18–21
  skills, 23–48
  styles, 153–4
  used as, 15
coaching framework
  Key Phase I, 3, 23, 78–105
  Key Phase II, 3, 23, 113–19
  Key Phase III, 3, 23, 120–30
  Key Phse IV, 3, 23, 130–4
  Step 1, 3, 56–76
  Step 2, 3, 77–105
  Step 3, 3, 106–34
coaching versus
  consultants, 9
  mentoring, 8
  therapy/counselling, 7
  training, 9

collude, 19
collaboration, 22
commissioning, 14–15
  1st/3rd party, 56, 66
communication, 24, 39–42
compassion, 53
confidentiality, 14, 79, 80–1, 118,
  142
  breaking, 82–3
curiosity, 33, 37–8

day to day activities, 160
dependency
  signs of, 158–9
  tackling, 159
directive style, 12
DISC, 60–2, 128
'do', 161
diversity, 9–11

engagement, 78, 99–100
environment, coaching, 78–82,
  118
ethics and standards, 82–3, 168
executive coaching, 79, 195
expectations, managing, 56–7
external profession coach, 138–40

face to face coaching, 15, 80–1,
  83
facilitating, 23, 108
FAQ's, 163–4
finding, coach, 58–60
flexibility, 127–8
focus
  holding, 49
  maintaining, 79, 107
  primary, 85, 101–2
forms, coaching, 170–85

foundation, coaching, 20–1, 84–5

Galloway Tim, 135
geography, 25, 26, 81, 126
glossary, 193–200
goals, 80, 84, 101–2, 118
gremlins, 96, 98–9, 124–5
group coaching, 195
GROW model, 108

humour, 39, 41, 99

impact, 22
initial contact, 3–4, 68
inquiry, 34, 38, 131
interest, clients, 160
'Internal coach', 137
intruding, 29, 32–3
intuition, 29, 30–1

language, meaningful, 25, 27–8,
  118
learning and experience, 24,
  42–8, 122–3
learning
  barriers, 71–3, 100
  cycle, 121
  process, 112–13
  styles, 65–7
  3A's of re-learning, 123
life
  coaching, 79
  purpose, 93–4
  skills, 129
listening
  blocks to, 29
  levels of, 29–30
  levels of perceptions, 28–30
logical levels, 113–14

logistics, coaching, 83–4, 144
loose ends, 83–4

measurement, 149–51, 166–8
    organisational, 167–8
    personal, 166–7
meta/helicopter view, 108, 197
mentoring, 8–9, 148–9
Meyers Briggs, 60
models, coaching, 108–12

neuro-linguistic programming,
    28–30
niche coaching, 79
non directive style, 13
non-judgement, 22, 53, 80

OOPS, 127, 162
organisation coaching, 142
outcomes
    unattached, 127, 162
    well formed, 114–16

pacing, 25–6
peaks and plateaus, coaching,
    25–6
permission, asking, 25, 28
personal coaching, 198
personal qualities, 18–19
personal working styles, 62–4,
    128
personality styles, 60–2, 123–4
perspectives and choices, 43–5
planning, 23, 108
preparations, 116–18
    prep forms, 116–19
procrastination, 126–7
professionalism, 21–2, 58–9, 118
purpose

coaching, 67–9, 74–6
life, 78, 93–5

questions, 24, 33–5
    clients, 66–7
    inquiry, 33, 38, 131
    open/closed, 33, 35–6
    powerful, 34–5

rapport, 24–6
reality, 126–7
re-calibration, 43, 48
referring clients, 70–1, 73–4,
    82–3
reframing, 43, 45
relationship
    coaching, 57–8, 77, 79, 119
    design and logistics, 83–4
    foundation, 20
    sustainable, 23, 103, 108, 120–9
    learning, 127–9
requesting and challenging, 43,
    45–7
resources, 186–92
responsibilities and
    accountability, 199
responsibilities, coach/coachee,
    79, 83, 84, 103–4, 118, 132,
    161
reverse mentoring, 8

self management, 18, 52–4
    as professional coach, 52–3
    personal self care, 54
self sabotaging, 126–7
signposting, 53, 187–92
SMART, 101–2
special conditions, 84
sponsoring, 14, 78

springboard, 23, 77–80, 84, 104, 144
structures, 43, 47, 131
    creating, 89–92
styles, coaching, 77–80
supervision, 50–1
    self assessment, 51–2

telephone coaching, 15, 80, 83
terms and conditions, 84, 169–70
therapy, 7
three step model, 108–9
tips and traps, 158–62
toolkit, coaches, 170–85
training and development, coaches, 48–50

trust, 80–1

understanding, 78, 95–6, 118

VAK, 28
VALUE, 79, 85–101, 127, 129
values, 78, 86–8

WAIT, 163
wants and needs, of client, 58
welcome pack, 77
wheel of
    life, 89
    self care, 42, Fig. 13
    self management, 39, Fig. 12
working styles, 62–5